Eight Jewish Philosophers

In the Tradition of Personalism

BY

LEON D. STITSKIN

Professor of Jewish Philosophy, Yeshiva University

FELDHEIM PUBLISHERS
Jerusalem/New York
5740 (1979)

Published and Distributed by

PHILIPP FELDHEIM, INC.

96 East Broadway
New York, N.Y. 10002

◉

FELDHEIM PUBLISHERS LTD.

P.O.B. 6525
Jerusalem, Israel

BALSHON PRINTING & OFFSET CO.
480 SUTTER AVENUE   BROOKLYN, N.Y. 11207
Printed in the United States of America

Table of Contents

TO
MY DEAR CHILDREN AND GRANDCHILDREN
TO WHOM I HOPE TO HAND ON OUR UNIQUE
AND ENDURING TRADITION

RABBI LEON D. STITSKIN

● *Dr. Sol Roth*

The Jewish religious personality can express itself appropriately in two contradictory ways. One of these is represented in the divine command to Abraham לך לך "Get thee out" (Genesis XII, 1) on which Rashi comments להנאתך ולטובתך, for your pleasure and for your well being. Jewish life does provide the opportunity for personal satisfaction and individual happiness. The *mitzvot* fashion and enrich life. The other is expressed in another divine command received by Abraham התהלך לפני "Walk before me" (Genesis XVII, 1), on which Rashi comments הדבק בעבודתי, "cling to my service." The true servant of G-d is not concerned with pleasures and satisfactions. He does not seek personal rewards for his efforts. He is prepared to transcend his self, to subordinate it to a higher purpose, to identify himself with a larger and more noble objective and to derive satisfaction from the success of the causes to which he is committed.

One can find fulfillment in self-assertion; that is way of the man who has chosen the pursuit of well being. One can find fulfillment in self-denial; that is the way of the man who has opted for commitment.

Rabbi Leon D. Stitskin, of blessed memory, chose the path of commitment. It is this principle that inspired and drove him all the days of his life. It is this principle that illuminates his biography and explains his career.

He was a man with a passion—as is natural for one who is moved by the spirit of dedication. He was a philosopher of the rationalist variety; reason meant a great deal to him. Yet when he engaged in philosophic debate, he often dropped the objectivity and detachment that are so characteristic of the life of reason and argued with an enthusiasm and excitement that is natural to the man of passion. He literally lost himself in debate.

vii

He had a passion for the Jewish people and the State of Israel. In his early rabbinic days, he served as a rabbi in the city of Rochester. He was a power in the community and an irresistible force in movements that were dedicated to the defense of the Jewish community and the creation of a Jewish State. He fought anti-Semitism successfully and provided effective and inspiring leadership in behalf of Zionism. And whenever he spoke of Israel—privately or publicly—he did so with a passion whose dimensions were co-extensive with the total Jewish community.

He was a man who was genuinely dedicated to spiritual values. He displayed a certain contempt for the material goods of life. The man who has chosen the path of pleasure pursues the accumulation of wealth to assure his happiness and well being. The one who is inspired by commitment to the ideals of Jewish life recognizes material goods as essential to enable him to carry on with his dedicated labors but as possessing no intrinsic value.

He was a humble man and humility flows readily and easily from the posture of commitment. His humility was exhibited in sensitivity towards others. He was frequently prepared to accept greater harm to himself, if it was necessary to do so, in order to avoid inflicting lesser injury upon others. Notwithstanding his manifold achievements, the thought that he was in any way superior or more deserving was repugnant to him. He could not contemplate it.

He was a man of intense and unconditional loyalty—to Torah, to the people of Israel, to the state of Israel, to the institutions with which he was associated, for example, Yeshiva University. Loyalty also follows naturally from the spirit of dedication. In the Spring 1978 issue of *Tradition,* he wrote a rejoinder to a thesis advanced by a certain academician in which he argued that the Divine promise of the Holy Land to the people of Israel was unconditional. His argument was derived from biblical and rabbinic sources, of course, but one who knew him could detect in his exposition his own uncompromising and unconditional loyalty to the Jewish state.

He enriched the life of Yeshiva University. Students sought him out; they enjoyed his courses. He founded the Department of Publications and, over the years, arranged for the appearance of a number of volumes, some of them classics in their fields. He expanded Yeshiva University and gave it a concrete presence on the West Coast in the form of a Teacher's College in Los Angeles, a school over which he presided as dean for many years.

He was a prolific author. He wrote *Judaism as a Religion; Judaism as a Philosophy: The Philosophy of Abraham bar Hiyya; Jewish Philosophy: a Study in Personalism; Letters of Maimonides.* He was the editor of a number of volumes, the most important of which are *Studies in Torah Judaism* and *Studies in Judaica.* Prior to his passing, he was preparing for publication a new book on the minor Jewish philosophers which now appears.

His *magnum opus* was *Jewish Philosophy, a Study in Personalism.* It was an ambitious and systematic work, the result of many years of teaching at Yeshiva University. He was determined to prove that Jewish philosophy is not merely a response to cultural pressures and intellectual currents of the day, that it is not just an attempt to reconcile the teachings of Judaism with that which passed for wisdom in every generation. Jewish philosophy is the independent theoretical development of conceptions authentically Jewish. It consists of an exposition of views concerning the nature of man and his place in the universe that are characteristically Jewish and implicit in biblical and rabbinic sources.

He argued that man is central in Jewish philosophic schemes, not in the sense that he is ultimate, as is the case in humanistic thinking, but in the sense that he is basic and fundamental. The entire system of Jewish thought which encompasses metaphysics, epistemology, ethics and theology begins with and is based upon its conception of man. He was fond of quoting a phrase popular in medieval philosophy.

דע את עצמך ואחר כך דע את בוראיך

"Know yourself and then you will know your creator."

He stressed the boundless potential of the human being for spiritual growth, moral development and intellectual achievement, and man's responsibility to engage in a constant, never-ending struggle to realize the possibilities within himself. And, for him, this was not merely a philosophic conception; it was a practical principle that guided his career. He was creative in the realm of Judaism, in both practical and theoretical ways, all the days of his mature life.

He was a dedicated teacher, a moving preacher, an inspiring leader, a profound thinker and an extraordinary human being. May his life be bound up everlastingly with the lives of his students, friends and descendants.

FOREWORD

● *Dr. Sidney B. Hoenig*

This volume, written by Dr. Leon Stitskin, is published post-humously. The prologue was penned by him in July 1978 but just before the High Holy Days in September he was stricken and on November 3, 1978 breathed his last, leaving in addition to this book many other philosophic works in manuscript form.

Dr. Stitskin may be characterized as *ish ha-eshkolot*—a man of divine qualities and vocations. He was an outstanding preacher, having occupied pulpits in Warren, Ohio; Rochester, N.Y.; and Philadelphia, Pa. But more than a decade, in the last years, he served as the Rabbi of the Yeshiva University Synagogue and officiated on the High Holy Days in the Lamport Auditorium of the University.

His main interest was the pursuit of philosophy and he developed the concept of personalism in Jewish life. Though many held and still hold that Jewish philosophy is merely a borrowing from classical and medieval studies, Professor Stitskin stressed emphatically that "Personalism maintains that Jewish philosophy is a genuinely independent creative scheme organically Hebraic and typically Jewish." Students of Jewish philosophy have always probed the major philosophers and in a sense ignored the minor coterie. To his credit Dr. Stitskin "resurrected" the minor Jewish medieval philosophers; this is the burden of this volume. In his perception, personalism is the unique aspect of Jewish philosophy because it "puts the mark of emphasis on the human potential and insists that man is neither a tragic creature nor a perfect being . . . personalism posits a realm of the spirit where the self exists in an undefined, functional and developmental situation . . . personalism maintains that the most essential values are to be found only in personal choice and self-fulfillment." Dr. Stitskin was so imbued with this philosophy of personalism that one may often find re-iteration of the many complex facets therein—especially in the

realm of self identification or seeking affinity ultimately with the
Divine Essence. Stitskin stressed that ". . . To be human in the
personalistic sense, is to be potentially divine. Personalism summons
us again to recover meaning for human existence and to reject a
mechanistic view of reality . . . every person is sacred because the
divine potential is present in him. . . ." No loftier interpretation
of one's mortal being could be enunciated.

Though Professor Stitskin immersed himself in philosophy he
was a pragmatic individual. It was he who founded the Yeshiva
University Press; the first book by the late President of Yeshiva
University, Dr. Samuel Belkin, was published by this press under
his aegis as Editor. As a teacher and administrator his qualities
were vast. The presence of Yeshiva University on the West Coast
—the formation of its Teachers College in Los Angeles—was the
result of his personal efforts. He spent months there organizing,
raising funds, administrating and teaching. Thus he was also the
ner ma'arvi, the "light of the West."

Dr. Stitskin's love for Israel too was immeasurable. No matter
how involved he was in various other activities, the eternity and
security of Israel always stimulated him. He was close to many
high officials—Senators and communal leaders—and if he felt that
they lacked any outspoken love for Israel, he did not refrain from
chiding them and bringing them to the realization of the magnitude
of Israeli continuity. He did this both verbally and in many written
communications. His hope was to walk the length and breadth of
Israel, to enjoy his last years there in study and reflection, but alas,
he was not granted this wish of permanent settlement but only of
being eternally laid to rest in holy ground of Israel.

If "personalism" and "ish ha-eshkolot" always stimulated him
scholastically and pragmatically, these elements likewise were
integrated into Dr. Stitskin's own personality. He was warm-hearted,
always paying heed to the ears of his students or rabbinic friends
who so often called upon him for guidance—whether it was for

philosophic research or problems in their communities. Hence, Stitskin, as the Rabbis' rabbi, often became the conciliator between rabbi and congregation. He was the confidant of Dr. Belkin throughout the arduos years of the latter's presidency and sought to alleviate for him the difficulties that that office demanded. Dr. Stitskin regarded Martin Buber, Gershon Churgin as well as Israel Efros and Joseph Soloveitchik as his teachers and mentors in philosophy and often would he mention the discussions he used to have with these scholastic giants. In addition to his editorial work as head of the Yeshiva University Press, he served as Associate Editor of the renowned orthodox journal "Tradition." Many of the articles on the minor philosophers first saw light in this publication but are here amplified. In the realm of practical rabbinics, he was also very active in the New York Board of Rabbis, and the Rabbinical Council of America, always ready to serve his fellowmen when called upon. Rarely did he show anger; his modesty was well known—even to a sense of timidity—but this was his humility —a result of his personalism and personality. Never did he shrink any duty or request—to aid his colleagues unselfishly.

The exceptional contribution by Dr. Stitskin in this volume is his analysis and philosophical evaluation of the minor philosophers and his demonstration that their studies also influenced the major Jewish philosophers whose teachings he probes in his last chapter. Each of the minor philosophers had a particular perspective but throughout the philosophy of personalism is very apparent:

1. Isaac Israeli stressed "the understanding of the purpose of the union in man of body and soul. . . . The striving of man is to imitate the divine by actualizing his potential."

2. Bahya Ibn Pakuda affirmed that "from the *Olam Katan* —the microcosm, the human species which is the ultimate purpose of the existence of the larger world, we derive evidence of Divine wisdom and design in all creation."

3. Abraham bar Hiyya attempted "to find a religious explanation of the whole process of history by establishing an exact correspondence between world eras and the days of creation. . . . Also, our existential situation will draw us into the unfoldment of ultimate truth, beholding the Transcendent from man's perspective in a two-fold aspect, God-in-Essence and God-in-Relation."

4. Joseph Ben Zaddik asserted that "when man actualizes himself he is nearer to God. For God's nearness or aloofness is conditioned by man's self-realization."

5. Moses Ibn Ezra insisted that "knowledge of God's perfect unity depends on man's perspective. It is from the human frame of reference that a determination is made whether essence and attribute are one."

6. Abraham Ibn Ezra taught that "our observances of the precept of the Torah are not for the sake of God but for our self perfection. . . . The supreme emphasis is to know one's own soul. For only as the soul first knows itself will it ultimately know the Creator. . . . In his self knowledge man becomes aware of his possibilities and these, in turn, imply his responsibilities."

7. Shem Tob Ibn Falaquera demonstrated that "knowledge and intellectual excellence is more than a mere search for truth. It is a means of ecstatic union of the human spirit with the divine spirit. Religious observances designed as a discipline to curb our animal impulses, pave the way for our intellect and pure spirit to conceptualize and contemplate the ultimate truths of philosophy."

8. Hillel ben Shmuel taught that "since the soul constitutes the very essence of man, any erroneous conception of man's essence might lead to false notions about the universe and even God himself."

Not satisfied with analysis and evaluation of these minor philosophers, Professor Stitskin prepared careful translations of important sections of these philosophers' writings so that they could speak for themselves and be fully comprehended from the original source. Hence he also prepared the Hebrew text in order that any student or reader could acquaint himself with the primary citation.

But even this was not sufficient for the careful scholar that Dr. Stitskin was. He portrayed in a definitive manner that "the minor Jewish philosophers are the key to an understanding of the major Jewish philosophers" and therefore, examining again these giants, he demonstrated some components of personalism such as, "the nature of man as a potential for good and evil." As enunciated by Saadia, Ibn Gabirol tended toward "the comparison of God's relationship to the world to that of man's soul and body," and stressed that knowledge of God's unity depends on man's perspective." Maimonides too devoted attention to "man's intellectual apprehension as linked to the divine intellect. . . . The attributes *zelim* and *demuth* in a logical sense apply equally to God and man." Likewise, Gersonides in "his treatise on the psychology and the immortality of the soul posits the leitmotif of his philosophy (again personalism)." Hasdai Crescas, likewise described man "as a composite of all existence. . . . Everything was subject to the rule of his wisdom as well as to the Divine rule."

In this manner the full thread of Dr. Stitskin's "Philosophy of Personalism," woven into the teachings of the minor and major Jewish philosophers, is perceptible. In his notes, however, he took careful cognizance of the ancient Greek philosophers as Aristotle, Plato, Philo as well as later teachers as Averroes, Thomas Aquinas, Spinoza, Hume, Kant and many others. Acquaintance with the Arabic philosophers and their teachings is evident in the citations from many giants of philosophy of the modern age. Professor Stitskin aimed in this work to be all-embracing and thorough, to prove his points of the philosophy of personalism as a Jewish scheme of investigation of man's place in this world.

Dr. Stitskin dedicated this volume, written when he had the stream of life within him, to his children and grandchildren with the hope "to hand on our unique and enduring tradition." Now that he is no more among the living the dedication becomes a three-fold one —a) to his own offspring b) to his students and readers— concerned with the pristine glory and meaning of Jewish philosophy and finally, the dedication becomes an *In Memoriam*—a memorial and tribute to the author who so devotedly immersed himself in Jewish philosophy and learning, in order to bequeath to the future a better understanding of our great intellectual and traditional heritage.

May the memory of Dr. Stitskin always be a source of blessing and an example of the true student—the *talmid hakham* who was vitally concerned with *Torah u-Madah,* Torah and general knowledge. This last phrase is the emblem of Yeshiva University wherein Dr. Stitskin served as teacher and administrator for decades; it also symbolizes his full activity and works. His scholarship, communal devotion and friendship will long be remembered.

I

PROLOGUE

An examination in this treatise of eight medieval Jewish philosophers reveals that personalism is the authentic unique Hebraic philosophic mode of discourse. The common refrain of the Jewish philosophers is that "philosophy is self-knowledge" (*ki ha-pilosophia hi ha-karat ha-adam et nafsho*) "and know yourself and then you will know your Creator" (*da et atzmekha v'ahar kakh teida et Boraikha*). Human personality constitutes the frame of reference for all inquiry. While in other philosophical schemes, a consideration of man's role in the cosmos is peripheral, in Jewish philosophy it is the all-illuminating core of its system. This notion is not based on some slanted interpretations of our speculative pursuits, but on well-documented evidence as articulated explicitly by the eight Jewish philosophers who, to my mind, are the key to an understanding of all Jewish philosophers.

Accordingly, what makes a Jewish philosophy Jewish is the formulation of propositions making claims about reality in personalistic terms. In our philosophical pursuit we begin from where we are, from our own subjectivity, and proceed to respond on the level of human experience to the eternal challenge of the unique content of reality which we share with God. The response varies with the developmental components of the human condition. In the initial stages of our developmental process, the self beholds the Divine Presence as a challenge to self-authentication and proceeds in an evolutionary thrust toward the development of a self-identifying activity of consciousness. In the ultimate situation, the self is in knowledge a principle of unification establishing a cognitive affinity with

1

God as the Transcendent, the absolute unity beyond all categories. By the same token, the nature of the Transcendent is experienced, at first, from the personalist point of departure, as causality (God-in-Relation) and, in the later stage, as God-with ideal ends, the difference between causality and substance in the idealistic sense, which identifies God with the essence of being, disappears.

Moreover, an exploration into the nature of man as the leitmotif of the Hebraic intellectual scheme gives legitimacy to Jewish philosophic inquiry. An examination of the human condition as the starting point of our speculative pursuit—unlike a consideration of abstract religious doctrinal beliefs—requires no antecedent presuppositions or preconceived notions. As Bar Hiyya points out, "When Scripture has completed the account of man's creation, it starts anew to delineate metaphysical issues in another form and in a different perspective" (*Megillat ha-Megalleh*, p. 60). The focus on human personality as a primary datum gives legitimacy to the Hebraic scheme to exercise those essential functions of philosophy— the criticism of commonly received opinions, and the disavowal of *a priori* proofs, which imply that their conclusions are assumed in the very statement of the argument.

Furthermore, the personalistic scheme propounded by our classical philosophers is indigenous to our biblical and rabbinic traditions and is, at the same time, contemporaneously meaningful and responsive to the perennial universal claims of the philosophical enterprise. This does not mean that our classical philosophers have not incorporated into their ideological construct categories from other systems. As long as the central core of personalism was stressed, Jewish philosophers had no hesitation to make use of other modes of thoughts to reinforce and validate their leitmotif.

Admittedly, the espousal of a philosophy of personalism as the unique scheme of thought in Judaism marks a departure from the standard notions, promulgated by our historians of ideas, that Jewish philosophy is a pale imitation of other philosophic schemes attempting to harmonize faith and reason. In this context, the avowed aim of objective scholarship as pursued by modern Jewish scholars and reflected in the *Wissenschaft des Judentums* was to account for every doctrine of a given Jewish philosopher as an appropriation from sources external to Judaism. Under these circumstances it is no wonder that not a single concept of original, unfossilized, philosophic thinking emerged from this school. Every notion was to be traced to someone who came before and very often with nothing to say to the modern world.

In a personalistic framework, however, which projects Jewish philosophy as a genuinely creative scheme organically Hebraic and typically Jewish, philosophic scholarly pursuits assume a new role. The aim of the new research consists in attempting to relate every area of investigation of a given philosopher to the central core and the principal thrust of our philosophic inquiry. While the Jewish philosopher may have appropriated philosophical materials that were widely extant before his time, the primary role of the personalistic scholar is to interpret the material in personalistic terms. Research of the sources of the categories in a given philosopher is peripheral to the task of attempting to identify them with the leitmotif of personalism. This is, in keeping, with the true nature of extension of knowledge, which is marked by three forms. On is teaching, which by itself does not increase our body of knowledge but which does extend the population of communicants. A second is scholarship, by which we mean development of rearrangements of an existing body of knowledge so as to give new insights. The third is research, by which new knowledge is acquired. The interplay of scholarship and research is especially true in a personalistic framework, where the categories of personality as basic structural features of reality, are the elements of an ontology more fundamental and revealing than traditional metaphysical categories. They unlock the door to the inner mystery of existence and the basic aspects of ultimate reality.

Finally, personalism as expounded in my major work, *Jewish Philosophy: A Study in Personalism,* embraces a methodology, a metaphysics, an epistemology, and an ethic in its conceptual as well as in its religious components. Its methodology projects the existential stance of the individual, the level of human experience, instead of some external premises emanating from on high, as the starting point and the frame of reference for all inquiry.

Its metaphysics delineates man as a potential, a self-identifying activity of consciousness to be actualized by constant involvement with life's experiences, and a process of conceptualization when ideas are transformed from being mere copies of phenomena to becoming ultimate purposes. It posits a realm of the spirit wherein the self exists in an undefined, developmental situation, reflecting a dialectic in the evolving human condition which requires moral freedom and an independent, inner-directed motivation in the valuational sphere, and intellectual identification with Ultimate Reality in the conceptual dimension. In his self-knowledge, man becomes aware of his possibilities which, in turn, make him a locus of responsibilities. To be human, in the personalistic sense, is to be potentially divine. As such he is driven to live in consciousness of responsibility and challenge to realize his potential. Reflecting on the divine potential present in him, he is constantly laden with a sense of obligation to move from a state of potentiality to a state of actuality, from what he is to what he ought to become. The authentic self grasps its own life as an existential demand of its finitude for the ultimate.

Clearly, then, in the personalistic context, reality is experienced in anticipation. It resides in a growth process, in an evolutionary thrust, and in a relational condition denoting a "not-yet" ontology which creates its own verification.

By the same token, the eminent theologian, Karl Heim, in his book *The Transformation of the Scientific World View* (New York, Harper & Bros.) supports the functional character of reality by tracing the disintegration of the "absolute object," in the phenomenal world which both classical and modern materialism assumed and which has disintegrated under the view of modern science into a field of radio-magnetic activity. The realm of Euclidian geometry and of Newtonian physics has given way to Einstein's "space-time relativity," and Hume's skepticism about the concept of causality has been supported by the skepticism of modern scientists whether the so-called "laws of nature" do not merely describe probabilities.

To be sure, the debate among scientists about determinism and indeterminism has not seriously affected the status of predictability as a test of truth in the natural sciences. The natural sciences are able to make repeated experiments under controlled conditions the basis of conclusions and predictions. But it may well be that the modern scientists have uncovered the mystery of creativity beyond and above the causal sequences which the scientists chart. This conclusion leads Karl Heim to the assertion that modern developments in the natural sciences have not persuaded the scientists that the so-called "methods of science" are as relevant as a sources of wisdom in human life as they are in the observation of nature.

Its epistemology is grounded in subjective truth. The objective reference of thought is interpreted from the standpoint of the subject rather than the object. Rather than have a reflection of the object, it is the subject who objectifies his thought. It is the existential self that imbues thought with objectivity. In self-knowledge and self-experience there is an identity of idea and object. The conscious mind, in the very act of knowing, is itself the reality. The deepest dimensions of human existence reveal the most fundamental aspects of ultimate reality. The acquisition of true knowledge is attained when one stakes all of his being to penetrate his life with concepts and essences, setting forth the conditions for self-authentication which create their own verification. While in the early stages of one's development the truths of reason are true by definition like mathematical axioms or intutitive apprehension, in the subsequent evolvement of one's inner world, reason assumes a new dimension denoting "the life of reason" and the appeal is to an epistemological monism. In the initial developmental process, the validity of knowledge must remain an assumption; in its consummative stage, the identification of thought and object is the guarantee of its validity.

Accordingly,subjective thinking does not imply, as some suggest, an epistemology without discipline or control. On the contrary, there is no other way of being objective than by starting from one's subjectivity. Subjective thinking, existential knowledge seeks to make sense of existence, of one's own existence. It strives to give a personalist answer to man's question about his own nature and awaken us to our authentic human situation. Consequently, the personalist thinking which is adequate to existence is a thinking of involvement and concern in what is thought about. It is thinking in which a man makes his decisions, affirms his commitment and ventures everything on it. The most essential human values are to be found not in knowledge of man as object or thing, endlessly explorable in his objectivation, but in the apperception of man in the totality of what he is and can become on the infinite road of his freedom and transcendence.

Its ethics denotes that moral freedom is not a gift bestowed but an achievement earned. The tensions involved between heteronomous and autonomous set of values are resolved in the personalistic focus on man's moral self-realization. As we discover the meaning of our existence and authenticate ourselves we evolve morally from "a push from without to a pull from within ethics." In the immediate situation of man's developmental process, ethical guidelines externally imposed are required. In the ultimate situation, ethical judgments are the expressions of the rational character of moral cognition coinciding with the divine Will.

In selecting eight medieval lesser known Jewish philosophers, among several others I examined in "Tradition" over the past twelve years, I had in mind those philosophers of the medieval period who, in my opinion, are the key to an understanding of the major Jewish philosophers. I have prefaced the translations of the texts of each philosopher's work with my introduction followed by notes and the Hebrew texts. In this work I have attempted to elaborate upon my introductions and my translations of the philosophers' texts which have appeared in "Tradition" in abridged forms.

Finally, I wish to express my indebtedness to Dr. Walter Wurzburger, editor of "Tradition", for granting me permission to republish them in book form. I am especially grateful to my dear wife, Dorothy, for her encouragement and my able secretary Frieda Spielvogel for her devoted efforts.

LEON D. STITSKIN.

July 2, 1978

II

WHAT IS JEWISH ABOUT JEWISH PHILOSOPHY

THE "MINOR" JEWISH PHILOSOPHERS

A General Introduction

The Jewish philosophy of Personalism embraces two dimensions: an historical and a conceptual. Its components are of a pure philosophic and of a religious nature.

A

The Historical Schema

Historically, personalism's basic thrust focuses on what is Jewish about Jewish philosophy. This book is a sequel to my major work, *Jewish Philosophy*: *A Study in Personalism,* and attempts to further substantiate my central thesis of Personalism by projecting the common refrain echoed by eight Jewish philosophers that "a definition of philosophy is man's knowledge of himself" (*Ki ha-pilosophia hi yediat ha-adam et atzmoh*) and "know thyself and then you will know thy Creator" (*da et atzmekha v'ahar kakh teida et Boraikha*). The ideological structure of the so-called minor Jewish philosophers is, thus, a key to an understanding of the major philosophers, like Saadia, Maimonides, Gersonides and Crescas.

Clearly, the terms *minor* and *major* philosophers, as in the case of the minor and major prophets, is used in a quantitative

and not in a qualitative sense. The usage of the terms has
nothing to do with the quality of the work but with the value of
output. Some philosophers enter into lengthy discussions, adorn
their style of writing with rhetorical flourishes or copious quotations from the Bible and Talmud, or incorporate in an eclectic
manner other systems and permit intrusion of other ideological
constructs, in order to present a compendium of science, metaphysics, theology, ethics, and epistemology. But the "minor"
philosophers eliminate adornments of language and other
systems of thought in order to project an authentic point of view
in a direct, concise, lucid, forthright manner. This is exactly
what Bar Hiyya did in his *Hegyon-ha-Nefesh* and *Megillat
ha-Megalleh,* as did the other minor philosophers. They
took the categories of Aristotle or neo-platonic or kalamistic
notions and applied them not to the latter's physics, metaphysics,
or logic but to their own central thesis of *Torat ha-Nefesh,* a
study of man's soul. Accordingly, every minor philosopher
defines philosophy either explicitly or implicitly as a study of the
nature and destiny of man.

   In our histories of Jewish philosophy, we often project
Jewish philosophy as a pale imitation of other modes of thought,
and Jewish philosophers as apologetics, eclectics, accepting out-
right some ready-made non-Hebraic formulations and clothing
them in a Hebraic garb. At best, philosophy is made out to be
an intermediary between Jewish tradition and other world-views,
or a rationalization of doctrinal beliefs. Personalism maintains
that Jewish philosophy is a genuinely independent creative
scheme organically Hebraic and typically Jewish. Its intellectual mode of discourse is articulated in an authentic Hebraic
world-view, grounded in the human condition as the point of
departure for all philosophic inquiry, and human personality
as the focus of our concern and the key to reality.

This thesis is not based on sentiment flattering to the "pride of the Jews,"[1] or on some slanted interpretations of philosophic notions, or on biblical exegesis but on well-documented sources as expounded by the classical philosophers. Admittedly, some modern Jewish philosophers like Moses Mendelssohn, Solomon Formstecher, Samuel Hirsch, Ludwig Steinheim and the 19th century founding fathers of the *Wissenschaft des Judentums* often failed to detect the basic thrust of the Jewish philosophic mode of discourse, because of their total preoccupation with examining the works of the major philosophers to the exclusion of the so-called minor philosophers. One is hard put to comprehend why no effort was made to reproduce critically the texts of the lesser known philosophers, even for the sake of rescuing them from oblivion, apart from their intrinsic value as a key to an understanding of the major philosophers. Commencing with the first Jewish dialectical philosopher, Isaac Israeli, an earlier contemporary of Saadia, and continuing through post-Maimonidean Shem Tov Falaquera and Hillel ben Shmuel, each philosopher defined the discipline as a study of the nature and destiny of man. As a matter of fact, it was this emphasis on human personality as a primary datum that brought Jewish philosophy back to its authentic organic character after a lapse of two centuries, beginning with Spinoza and ending with the Berlin period of Hermann Cohen. The central position of man as an end in himself of infinite realizable worth prompted Cohen to a synthesis of Judaism and reason as the source of reality, and paved the way for Rosenzweig's and Buber's authentic Hebraic mode of philosophic discourse.

Moreover, by projecting an all-illuminating principle of Judaism that is indigenous to our cultural and historical processes, we have eliminated two extreme, diametrically opposite approaches to speculative thought, prompted by the nature of Judaism as a religious culture and ideological construct always cast amidst a variety of strange and often conflicting currents of thought. First, there was the notion prevalent among the Jews of Alexandria in the first century before the common era, and given credence by the medieval philosophers, to the effect that the Jews were the original cultivators of philosophy, and that other nations, including the Greeks, owed their development in that discipline to the Jews. On the other hand, modern Jewish philosophers following Spinoza's notion that philosophy and religion are two distinct disciplines proceeded to promulgate one set of rules for thinking (philosophy) and another for value (religion). The categories and conceptual processes of one do not apply to the other. This conclusion became the basic assumption of almost every modern Jewish philosopher and was responsible for distorting the Hebraic scheme out of its authentic meaning and distinctive mode of discourse.

Personalism, on the other hand, by projecting a central affirmation, a leitmotif, a *merkaz nekudah* which became its organized principle of life, is designed to retain a clear pattern of Hebraic distinctiveness and at the same time of developing a process of integration with universal modes of discourse. In this context, there is no danger of appropriating categories from other disciplines that may seem extraneous to the basic Hebraic scheme, as long as we intellectualize to the point of supporting the all-illuminating core that is our own, and is at work through all the stages of philosophic speculation. By the same token, we have eliminated a basic problem of the legitimacy of the inquiring mind in a religious philosophical mode of discourse. By projecting human personality as the point of departure for all inquiry, we have initiated an area of investigation wherein

we may philosophize without preconceived notions and antecedent presuppositions. Abraham bar Hiyya states in the
opening remarks of his philosophical treatise *Hegyon ha-Nefesh*
(p. 2) that the scriptural verse "'From my flesh shall I behold
God' (Job 19:26) gives us permission to investigate the views
of the classical philosophers and their theories of creation."

Admittedly, if the essential distinguishing marks of a sound
philosophic method are to avoid drawing conclusions from
preconceived presuppositions, and to analyze critically a given
proposition by examining alternatives to its supporting evidence,
then personalism emerges as the authentic Hebraic philosophic
scheme in keeping with the tradition of the Judaic *Weltan-
schauung* and *daat ha-Torah*. Abraham bar Hiyya addresses
himself to this question when he begins his philosophical
inquiry by probing an apparent contradiction in Scriptures regarding the nature of man. One scriptural verse glorifies man,
exclaiming, "Thou hast given him dominion over the works of
Thy hands, everything hast Thou placed beneath his feet" (Ps.
8, 7); while the other tends to demean his stature, saying, "how
much less the son of earth the mere maggot" (Job 25, 6).
Hence, by examining the alternatives in personalism, already
alluded to in Scriptures, one may legitimately embark upon a
philosophic investigation without unquestioning presuppositions
and antecedent affirmations.

B

The Conceptual Dimension

Clearly, the principle thrust of our conceptual framework
is human personality. The primacy of man is the point of
departure for all inquiry, ethical judgment and cognitive appre-

hension. The key to an understanding of the ultimate reality
of existence lies in the study of the nature and destiny of man.
The accent in Jewish thought is on Personalism. It is on the
level of human experience that we respond to the eternal
challenge of the unknown. It is from the perspective of man's
frame of reference that a determination is made whether the
response is of an analytical or a poetic, synoptic nature. The
human condition, the existential situation, sets in motion relationships with the unknown, the phenomenal world and the
social structure.

THE NATURE OF MAN

But what is the nature of man? Theological notions in
the West, grounded in ancient mythological beliefs of grim
fatalism, depicted man as a tragic creature, born with irremediable inadequacies and unregenerate depravity. By nature
perverse and helpless, man is unable to pull himself up by his
own capacities, but must rely solely on grace conferred upon
him as a gift for his unquestioning faith. Such a culture, thus,
defies the reality of progressive organic intellectual and spiritual
development, and expresses contempt for human nature and
scorn for man's limitless potentialities.

On the other hand, predominant Eastern doctrines delineated man as a "finished product" endowed with a "field of
consciousness" of consummate creative intelligence and energy.
To find fulfillment in an expanded consciousness, it was assumed,
one had to tap only one's own inner resources, which it regarded
as a microcosmic actualized realm of awareness, a complete
"ideal order," which each person possesses innately, making
him free with the freedom of being open to oneself. No links
to the external empirical world were necessary for generating

creative energy; only total concentration upon one's inner world. A counterpart of this scheme in Western society appeared in the nineteenth century romantic and secular humanistic schools, which projected man as the tough-minded egotist, the heroic figure whose abundant wisdom and creative power, born of the advances in our technological skills, would replace the omniscience and omnipotence of the Deity.

The difficulty with either system is that one denies the human potential altogether, while the other posits man as an actualized self, who is the sole source of creative intelligence and power. Personalism, on the other hand, puts the mark of emphasis on the human potential and insists that man is neither a tragic creature nor a perfect being. It delineates man as a potential to be realized by constant involvement with empirical and ideological experiences. The absoluteness of self, oriented by self-transcendence and a growth process of soul-making, creating its own verification, constitutes the central core of the personalistic scheme.

The notion of man as a potential is attested to by biblical, rabbinic and philosophic traditions. The biblical delineation of the creation of man in the divine image (*zelem elokim*), is an endowment in a state of potentiality to be actualized when man stakes his existence on the penetration into his being of concepts, essences, and empirical experiences. Every person is sacred because this divine potential is present in him, and at the highest level of his possibilities he is truly a mirror in which we can see reflected the unique content of reality, which he shares with God.

Our sages in the Talmud seem to attest to the fact that the entire corpus of Jewish law — the written and oral law — was intended not solely as a document for prescribing ethical and ceremonial practises and laws, but equally as an exposition to be studied and analyzed in order to develop our potential intellectual faculty for self-authentication. Otherwise, how explain the rabbinic notion that two contradictory decisions are equally valid since both emanate from the same Living God— *ilu v'ilu dibrei elokim hayim.* But what is even more puzzling is the assumption that two opposing views can proceed from one Source of Truth. However, if the focus of our concern in studying Torah is not solely on reaching legal decisions but on speculative explorations into the reasons for the opposing decisions, then, in order to cultivate our intellectual faculty for self-authentication, it is quite plausible for contradictory statements to emanate from one Source of Supreme Thought.

This is surely the implication of the rabbinic observation with reference to the biblical verse introducing the Decalogue: "'And God spoke all these words' (Exod. 20:1). One will perhaps say, that since some render a decision of unclean and the others of clean; some prohibit and the others permit it; some declare it invalid and the others declare it valid, how can I learn the Torah? Therefore it is said . . . One God gave them and one master (Moses) spoke it from the mouth of the Lord of all creation, praised be He! . . . You must therefore make your ears like the hopper to receive the teachings, and *gain an understanding heart to comprehend the reason* why these declared it clean and the others unclean; why they prohibit and the others permit; why these declare invalid and the others valid" (T.B. Hagigah 3b).

As potential beings, we are given a Torah not only as a prescription of laws to follow, but as an exposition to analyze, to study and explicate in order to develop our human intellect.

Inasmuch as rationality is conferred by the divine mind, contrary decision and intellection over them may also provide the means for actualizing our potential rational faculty.

Consider, further, the rabbinic concept of *Periat baal hob Mitzvah* — "the debtor's return of a loan is regarded as a *mitzvah*" (T.B. Ket. 86a; B.B. 174a; Erukhin 22a). This notion of sublimating a simple legal act to a sacred deed has transformed an ordinary transaction, governed generally by the legal process to protect the interest of the creditor, into a higher moral purpose. It is indicative of the basic thrust of the entire corpus of the Hebraic judicial system which was directed toward the cultivation of man's developmental character rather than the mere protection of property. According to Maimonides, even *mitzvot bein adam l'Makom* (*mitzvot* concerning man's relation to God) tend "to regulate each man's actions which only concern man and lead him to perfection" (*The Guide*, 3, 35).

By the same token, Maimonides in the very first chapter of *The Guide* posits the primacy of man in the Bible as a development process by pointing out that the terms *zelem* and *demuth*, which have reference to the divine intellectual faculty were meant not to describe God's attributes but man's, in the sense of projecting man as possessing "as his proporium something that is strange, not found in anything else existing under the sphere of the moon, namely, intellectual apprehension. In the exercise of this, no sense, no part of the body, none of the extremities are used; and therefore this apprehension was likened unto the apprehension of God, which does not require an instrument, although in reality it is not like the latter apprehension but only appears so to the first stirrings of opinion" (*The Guide*, 1, 1). In *Sefer ha-Mada*, "Hil. Teshuba" 5, 2,

Maimonides further states: "Let not the notion expressed by
foolish and senseless folk among you pass through your mind
that at the beginning of a person's existence the Almighty
decrees that he is to be either righteous or wicked. This is not
so. Every human being may become righteous like Moses, our
teacher, or wicked like Jeroboam; wise or foolish, merciful or
cruel, niggardly or generous, and so with all other qualities . . .
Thus Jeremiah said 'out of the mouth of the Most High, pro-
ceedeth not evil or good' (Lam. 3, 38); that is to say, the
Creator does not decree either that a man shall be good or that
he shall be wicked."

REALITY

In this context, reality resides in a growth process of soul-
making, an evolutionary thrust, a transcendental situation, a
relational condition as man evolves from a state of potentiality
to a state of actuality; from what he is to what he ought to be.
Reality is experienced in anticipation, in suspense. It is futuristic, corresponding to the prophetic *ahrit ha-yamim* (the end
of the days), a "not-yet" ontology. Unlike the early Greek
natural philosophers who speculated on a primary substance,
or the mechanistic naturalists who conceived atoms like little
bits of matter resembling billiard balls, or light consisting of
waves moving through space like ripples in a pool, personalism
posits a realm of the spirit where the self exists in an undefined,
functional, developmental situation. To be sure, the assumption
in modern science[2] of a relational conception of the original
structure of experience is corroborative of the personalistic
notion of the relational as distinguished from the atomistic theory
of consciousness.[3]

But, in truth, the transformation, under the view of modern

science of the classical, materialistic notion of the "absolute object" into a field of radiomagnetic activity—as well as the contemporary scientific notion of shattering every view of the world as a closed and complete whole—has done more than to support the functional character of reality in personalism. It has underscored also the inadmissability of the system of nature as the ultimate source of meaning for our lives. It is a characteristic of the greatness of modern science that it comprehends its own limits with regard to supplying us with the aims of life. By virtue of its very clarity, scientific knowledge directs us elsewhere for the sources that support the free exercise of personal existence. As against the objectivists trends of viewing man as a thing, ignoring his free existence as it is lived from the inside, personalism maintains that the most essential human values are to be found only in personal choice and self-fulfillment. The efficiency of our social structure must be judged in terms of the free existence it supports. Such existence, of course, cannot be produced and organized mechanically. The individual must win it for himself. In such a futuristic ontology, man is led, not only to an authentication of the unique content of reality within him, but to an awareness of a Being which both transcends him and touches him very deeply.

Clearly, in personalism, man's encounter with Ultimate Reality is of a twofold nature: in the realm of the immediate situation and in the ultimate situation. In the immediate situation, as man strives for self-authentication, the truths or reason are true by definition like mathematical axioms. There is an openended intuitive compliance with the content of ethical and spiritual tenets.

In the realm of the ultimate situation, the self is, in knowledge, a principle of unification establishing a cognitive affinity with the Divine as the Transcendent, the absolute unity beyond all categories of existence. Beyond the ethical and spiritual experiences for self-authentication, in the final stage, as Martin Buber points out, is the "experience of the divine knowing . . ." This "is not like any experience of nature, it is a genuinely biographical experience, that is, what is experienced in the course of one's own personal life in destiny as it is lived through in each particular occasion" (*Good and Evil,* New York, Charles Scribner's Sons, 1953, p. 57).

By the same token, the emphasis in personalism on a two-fold encounter with ultimate reality has eliminated the so-called unbridgeable dichotomy between a quest for a rational faith and a non-rational submission to an authoritative tradition, a *Gefühlphilosophie.* While in the immediate situation non-rational elements in life as well as the central significance of commitment are crucial to a viable faith, in the ultimate situation the importance of the intellect and a logical assent in a vital faith are primarily determinative in internalizing religious affirmations and rendering them inner-motivated rather than externally imposed. As Saadia maintains that only a rationally substantiated faith renders it *emet berurah*—certain truth. He further states: "If both the scholar and student will follow this (the conceptual) path . . . the believer who blindly relies on tradition will turn into one basing his belief on insight and understanding" (Prolegomena to *Emunot v'Deot*). Even the presumably anti-rationalist Yehudah Halevi argues that a "skeptical soul will be content only after speculative investigation when, *subsequently,* knowledge and tradition combine and become one and the same" (Kuzari, 5, 1).

One of the classic issues of philosophy, the question of freedom and determinism, is likewise resolved in personalism by man's double encounter with reality. In the initial stage, human behavior is under the universal sway of determinism. Although contemporary scientific theories have offered explanations of events that seem to depart radically from the traditional conceptions of the causal relation we find in classical mechanics, no good reason has been put forward for believing that modern science does not continue to be deterministic in the important sense of the term. However, the Hebraic notion of determinism should not be confused with the idea of an inevitable fate, fatalism. We look upon causal laws as offering the conditions which make it possible for men to plan their lives with some assurance and to make the choices, paving the way to freedom in the ultimate state of man's development. Human freedom is not a gift bestowed but a goal achieved. A necessary element in the idea of freedom, in the ultimate situation, is a measure of determinism correctly understood in the immediate situation that sets the course for ultimate freedom.

A penetrating study, *Determinism And Freedom In the Age of Modern Science, A Philosophical Symposium,* edited by Sidney Hook (New York, New York University Press, 1958), reflects the classic spectrum of disagreements from strict determinism to the personalistic notion as delineated in my work *Jewish Philosophy: A Study in Personalism* on "The Ethics of Personalism."

AN ETHICAL, SPIRITUAL AND COGNITIVE PERSONALITY

Accordingly, in personalistic terms, the self is a self-identifying activity of consciousness involved in staking one's existence on the penetration into one's being of essences and empirical experiences. The focus of our concern is on the three-fold response to the challenge of self-authentication, on the valuational, spiritual and conceptual levels. The aim is to attain an ethical personality, a spiritual personality, and a cognitive personality.

As an ethical personality, in the valuational sphere, man employs discursive reason (*reshit hokhmah yirat Hashem* — "the first principle of reason is reverence for God" [Ps. 111, 10])[4] as an instrument for moral freedom, as he advances from an external to an inner-directed motivation. By striving to unify our will with conviction, ethical judgments receive their sanction and validity by a "pull from within rather than a push from without."

As a spiritual personality, the experience of the human personality to transcend beyond himself draws him existentially to embrace doctrinal beliefs and religious hypotheses. The biblical notion of *zelem elokim,* which constitutes a component *sui generis* of Judaism, embraces both properties of seeking the highest good in the path of self-authentication and believing that it is realizable. Otherwise, the essential character of its nature would fall into a contradiction with itself.[5]

It should be noted, however, that initially we are drawn by the evolutionary thrust of our existential condition into adopting an open-ended approach, an unconditional, intuitive compliance with the content of religious doctrine for self-authentication. In the immediate situation one is required to venture the leap and stake one's whole existence on maximal practice, and it is only in the consummative stage when human reason actualized attests to the truths of doctrinal beliefs. Thus, in the early state of man's evolvement, the truths of reason are true by definition like mathematical axioms. In the subsequent development of one's inner world, reason assumes a new role of the "life of reason."

By the same token, revelation, accepted intuitively as a historical fact by the very nature of our human condition in the initial stages of self-development, constitutes a facet of the basic data necessary for the actualization of the faculty of reason. The revelatory material, which consists of first-hand expressions of religious apperceptions and fundamental facts of faith, forms the experiential basis for the development of the dictates of reason. Just as our knowledge of the physical world is based upon our sense experience, since human thought, empiricism would argue, can only deal with material which has been given in experience, so is our religious knowledge, in the incipient state of our rational development, grounded upon aspects of human experiences which are received by revelation. While in the early developmental process the validity of the revelatory act must remain an assumption, in the subsequent involvement of one's inner world, the authentication of the canons of reason within us provides existential certainty for the historic act of revelation. Otherwise the human condition would fall into a contradiction with itself, as the logical order of the mind corresponds to the universal truths embodied in the revelatory act.

Those two aspects of revelation are attested to by the double response of our people at Sinai, *naaseh v'nishma* — we shall do and we shall hear. The initial stage of our developmental process is characterized by *nasseh*, an intuitive compliance with religious practice. The consummative stage is depicted as *v'nishma*, and we shall hear. The act of hearing, it should be noted, is not a passive one. On the contrary, to hear is to engage in a creative effort of mental activity such as, thinking and knowing, willing and judging, questioning and assenting, interpreting and internalizing. It is an act of communication and in any process of communication there are two elements involved, the dispenser of speech and the recipient whose response is also decisive.

In my discussion on the methodology of personalism in *Jewish Philosophy—a Study of Personalism,* I maintain that Judaism which originated as a divine revelation endowed us with a creative power to interpret the law, to enact new laws within its own process, and to authenticate the law as one's own so that it becomes an element of one's religious conscious- ness. The nature of relevation is, thus, delineated in the Bible as an act of divine communication which depends not only upon the source of the sound but also upon the spiritual and intellec- tual authentication of the recipient.

At this stage the spiritual personality has blended into a single unity two fundamental issues of the philosophic enter- prise, namely, what can I know and what can I believe. Both issues are, crucial to the spiritual dimension which strives to make man at home in the universe by affirming with cognitive certainty his existence in the past, the present and the future— "I was, I am, and I shall be."

As a cognitive personality, in the conceptual sphere, personalism by positing a teleological idealism as the ultimate metaphysical generic characteristic of reality, actualized reason —*reshit hokhmah knei hokhmah,* "the first principle of reason is to acquire reason" (Prov. 4, 7); reason as a necessary idea of reason; a regulative principle expressing a demand for co- herent concepts when, by means of conceptualization, ideas work together—takes on an objective content, a world of its own, transforming ideas from being mere copies of phenomena to becoming ultimate purposes. As such, they structure an internalized ideal order relating the realities of its universal, unified concepts to the cosmic ideal order, and in the ultimate situation a cognitive identification with Ultimate Reality, the Divine Presence and Supreme Thought. Here again, while in the initial stage of the actualization of our potential, the self beholds the Transcendent as a challenge to the development of a self-identifying activity of consciousness, in the ultimate state, the self is in knowledge a principle of unification, establishing a cognitive affinity with the Divine. By the same token, the nature of the Divine, on the level of human experience, is viewed by the two metaphysical categories of relation —causality and teleological idealism.[6] The attributes of causality, as I pointed out in my book *Judaism As a Philosophy — A Study in Personalism,* point to God-in-Relation in the early stages of our evolvement. In the subsequent state of our actualization, we experience the Transcendent as the Universal Essence of Being, God-in-Himself, God-in-Essence (the Unknowable, the *Ein-Sof*). In this sense, the difference between the categories of relation and the fundamental problem of how to recognize our thoughts as being part and at the same time apart from an all-encompassing nature and Ultimate reality disappears.

Moreover, if the ultimate aim of man, according to Maimonides is *yediat Hashem* — "knowledge of God" — this can be attained by a process of self-authentication which leads to a knowledge of God. Martin Buber likewise asserted that "God does not wish to be defined, discussed, or defended by us, but simply to be realized by us."[7] For the ultimate issues of life, the existent individual's affirmed thought is decisive in establishing the best criteria of the truth of the objective content. Truth is not merely a statement of fact. The individual's actualized thought modes are truth. The growth process, the dynamic realizable scheme in which man is existentially involved creates its own verifiability. Instead of believing that certain facts are the case, it is primarily the realizability of certain conditions of self-authentication that brings about its own fulfillment. The realizable is the verifiable.

C

The Relevance of Personalism to Contemporary Issues

Now this scheme has many ramifications in a personalistic mode of discourse, which has given rise to a complete system of the speculative pursuit embracing a methodology, a metaphysics, an epistemology, an ethic and a psychology in a new perspective, grounded in the human condition. The conceptual implications inherent in this approach are far-reaching and constitute the burden of our area of investigation in my major work: *Jewish Philosophy: A Study in Personalism*. Additionally, however, the essentially unique formulations of personalism have a challenging impact on contemporary issues and the thought modes of our philosophical pursuits.

PHILOSOPHICAL AND THEOLOGICAL FORMULATIONS

For one thing, in contemporary philosophy, the attempt to relate all inquiry to a central thesis of the human condition has rescued the enterprise from being reduced, from an inquiry into a generic, pervasive characteristic of reality, a comprehensive world view, to a mere critical discipline of "talking about talking," the meaning and clarification of language.

More than 200 years ago, David Hume destroyed the cherished connection between reason and the empirical world in his essay, *A Treatise of Human Nature* (1739). Among other arguments, Hume claimed that it is folly to think any observed effect follows any cause by force of reason. If a rock is dropped, said Hume, it is custom and experience that tell us the rock will fall, not reason. A scientist could apply practical laws to describe the way a rock falls, but no philosopher could produce the pure reason why it had to be so and not otherwise. Hume showed that the truths of reason are true by definition, like mathematical axioms, but that the truths of the world we live in are based on experience instead of logic.

Hume's essay marked a turning point in the history of philosophy. By cutting reason off from the world, he undermined the hope that a searing rational mind could perfect an explanation of the entire universe. After Hume, notwithstanding the mighty labors of Immanuel Kant to rescue the philosophical force of pure reason from Hume's dilemma, philosophy has come to restrict the scope of its inquiries to coincide with the limits of reason. It has tended toward logic and mathematics, and it has intensified philosophy's concern with the meaning, structure and precision of language. This is analytic philosophy, which focuses on the tools of inquiry more intensely than on its objects, tending to eschew that which cannot be rigorously proved.

Over the last seventy-five years, analytic philosophy has come to dominate Western philosophy — first in England and now in the United States.

Such an attitude has turned the philosophic pursuit into a critical discipline, a sort of an intellectual busy-body with no home of its own but operating in every area of human endeavor wherever ambiguity and obscurity abound.

Personalism, on the other hand, by maintaining that the only knowledge worth having is knowledge that bears directly upon the human experience has restored the enterprise to its classical orientation as a distinct discipline. While the logical positivists may tell us that all ultimate questions are meaningless, personalism maintains that ultimate issues are at stake in our existence, the relevance of which surpasses all final formulations. Moreover, a definition of philosophy as a study of man's knowledge of himself does not circumscribe or limit the enterprise. On the contrary, philosophy, thus contrived, seeks the best possible interpretation of the world as we know it. But what is even more, it tends to expand the life of reason to the point where ideas are not only copies of phenomena but can become ultimate purposes. It projects a "not-yet" ontology — a reality experienced in anticipation, the absoluteness of self oriented by self-transcendence.

Its teleological idealism, as we indicated before, has made it possible to find a home for the enterprise by blending two major issues of philosophy, namely, how can I *believe* and how can I *know*. Once the starting point for our speculative pursuit is from where we are rather than from beyond there — to assert anything about the beyond at our initial stage of exploration is to jump off into the dark—we are on our way to self-awareness leading to an ultimate awareness of the Transcendent.

Admittedly, the three traditional theistic arguments by classical and medieval philosophers have been largely refuted and fatally weakened by the criticism of Hume and Kant, and by some contemporary philosophers. The existence of God is consequently not determined by probing the nature of the world (cosmological),[8] the nature of the world's design (teleological)[9] or the nature of God (ontological)[10] but by the nature of man.

The existence of God is derived not from external accepted premises but from one's experiential reality and existential condition. The pull is from within, existentially moving toward God rather than the push from without extending from God. We find the infinite, not by looking away from the finite self, but by looking more deeply into the finite self. To be human, in the personalistic sense, is to be potentially divine. Living is an experience which allows one a sense of unfoldment and fulfillment as one joins the inevitable evolutionary ascent toward a higher spiritual consciousness. The authentic self grasps its own life within a larger cosmic setting. It sees itself as part of a greater whole, as an existential demand of its finitude for the ultimate Reality. Our built-in hierarchical quality to transcend beyond ourselves necessarily draws us to affirm the Ultimate Transcendent.

ON A SOCIAL LEVEL

Moreover, on a social level, the type of society we envisage is determined by the kind of philosophy about man we espouse. If we stress man's essential depravity and his helplessness to save himself, we are undermining man's unique faculty to rationally structure his environment. Instead of fashioning a society that is designed to authenticate his developmental capacity, a doctrine of man's innate irremediable inadequacies inevitably creates a repressive social structure which reduces man to an abject puppet of the state, hopelessly deadlocked in a senseless social conformity and depersonalized collectivity. Our attitude toward man's nature and destiny determines whether man is the servant of the state or the state is a sociopolitical instrument designed to serve the developmental needs of the individual.

Clearly, a philosophy that expresses scorn for man's limit-less potentialities and contempt for human nature, submerges man in a totality of society's repressive measures, melting him down into a common mass. It is only when the mark of emphasis is on the generic problems of existing man and of his unique rational faculty for transcendence and unfoldment that we can envision a social structure designed to recover meaning for human existence, nourished by an environment that encourages the growth process of soul-making.

ON A PERSONAL LEVEL

On a personal level, the profound significance of personalism, further, lies in its protest against a definition of the real world in terms of impersonal, technocratic-scientific terms; that is, in its critique and radical rejection of the reigning mechanistic view of reality. It insists that human values belong to the real world, and that a good society has its basis, not in impersonal mathematical formulas, but in human sensibilities, in personal renewal and in the realm of the spirit. The deepest dimensions of human existence, mirroring the Divine image, reveal the most fundamental aspects of ultimate reality. Expounding upon the traditional metaphysical categories such as substance and causality alone cannot unlock the door to the inner mysteries of existence.[11] The qualities of human personality are the elements of a metaphysic that are basic to the structural features of reality. Indeed, the highest level of conceptualization consists in the formulation of propositions making claims about reality in personalistic terms.

Moreover, the evolutionary thrust built into the human condition requires a concretization in man's self-identifying activity of consciousness of the Divine imperative and the

generic and purposeful characteristics of reality by means of
the dialectical process. Delineating man as a potential to be
realized by constant involvement with empirical and ideological
experiences, personalism formulates a dynamic of an interactive
process of endowing our experiences and perceptual data with
our unique endowments by a corpus of Jewish Law and *mitzvot*
—designed to bring to each aspect of life the extraordinary
concern with form of the most gifted craftsman and the intensity
of the genius—and, subsequently, the objects of our experience,
in turn, help in the development of soul-making and the actualization of the soul's immortal core.

In the Hebraic framework, the practice of *mitzvot* and
intellection over them indirectly endows each aspect of our experience with a heightened value capable of actualizing our
potentialities and, in some instances, is almost comparable to a
direct process of conceptualization and intellectualization.

Inasmuch as *mitzvot* are rational, grasping their rationality
and intellection over them constitutes an integral part of their
observance and contributes also to the development of the
human intellect for the attainment of one's destiny. To be sure,
some reasons for the *mitzvot* may be readily comprehensible,
while others are accessible only to the few. But the search for
taame ha-mitzvot, as a search to fathom divine wisdom establishes patterns of thinking with life's experiences conducive to
come cognitively nearer to God. As I pointed out in my work
Judaism As a Philosophy (p. 6). "Every Biblical *mitzvah* is
related to some commanding purpose and its observance constitutes not a perfunctory performance but the concretization
and subsequent absorption of a cosmic design, a transcendental
content, and a metaphysical insight instrumental in the development of our psychic organ."

The crisis of our age, marked by an uncontrollable mechanical necessity and grounded in naturalistic empiricism, is man's alienation from the experiential world. Engulfed by this technological electronic society, we seem to have set up a colossal self-contained machine tending to leave us out of the scheme of things, and depriving us of the interactive process responsible for man's self-realization.

Prior to the machine age, even the ordinary craftsman of an artifact had a sense of creativity and personal enhancement by virtue of investing the object of his work with a personal endowment and, in turn, the finished product filled him with a sense of creativity and fulfillment. With the advance of technology, there emerged a senseless mechanistic conformity reducing man to an impersonal functionalism, tending to blur the edge of man's individuality.

When primitive man confronted for the first time the massive rocks that seemed so impregnable and invincible, he escaped to the caves. But as he began to recover his humanity, he emerged from the cave and commenced to engrave signs, letters and words upon the stones infusing them with his spirit and form. Personalism summons us again to recover meaning for human existence and to reject a mechanistic view of reality. By bringing our self to the knowing process, personalism maintains that the real world is not without human value. Without a certain kind of self-knowledge, our knowledge of the outside world is useless. This implies a constant involvement in life's experiences whereby we invest our unique endowments of a *zelem elokim.*

SECULAR EXISTENTIALISM AND PERSONALISM

Finally, personalism underscores a conceptual dynamic of self-realization motivated not by the tragic dimensions of life but by the unbounded possibilities inherent in man's soul as the creative act of God. Unlike secular existentialism which stresses alienation, sick despair, as the spur and motif for creative commitments, personalism projects the hierarchical thrust built into the structure of the existential condition as the motivation for self-authentication.

The secular existentialist has posited man in opposition to nature, formulating the notion of the separation of selfhood as alienation derived from the hostility of the environment and, at best, the neutrality of God, with which man can never cope. One is arrayed against the other in a spirit of hostility, living in a world which threatens to overwhelm man. To exist is to live under the threat of nothingness. The absurd is coexistent with life, and the nausea is the self's awareness of its sinking into the slime of the forces of imprisonment. The tragic aspect of the existential condition is the spur, the motivation, for self-authentication. It constitutes the motif for creative commitment in existentialism.

To Heidegger, as well, man is ontologically insecure. He is always in danger of losing his being, *Dasein*, to the *Verfallen*, a falling away into the nothingness of *alltaglichkeit*, or every-dayness. He can easily disappear into his contingencies, although, to Heidegger, man differs from plants and animals in that his existence is partly under his own conscious control.

In *Being and Nothingness,* Sartre summarizes the idea

behind existentialism in these words: "Man can will nothing
unless he has first understood that he must count on no one but
himself; that he is alone, abandoned on the earth in the midst
of his infinite responsibilities, without help, with no other aim
than the one he sets himself, with no other destiny than the
one he forges for himself on this earth." Separation, alienation,
is a metaphysical category[12] derived from the secular existentialist analysis of the human condition. It is the foundation of all
foundations, and to abolish it in a total reconciliation with
nature is to undermine personal existence itself. Existentialists
cannot accept the abstract universal of Kant or the concrete
universal of Hegel because, in the first place, man has no essence
whose destiny it is to engross all, and second, because the "all"
is not friendly to man.

For personalists, however, as indicated, the awareness of
separation is not ontological but psychological. It is only when
we become conscious of separate existence vis-a-vis the environment that our unique position as masters of the natural forces
is set in motion. Basic to man's hierarchical movement and
transcendental process is a necessary detachment from the presented stimuli and phenomenal data.[13] However, one is not
arrayed against the other in antagonism but in a mode of
challenge and response. God is omniscient, the universal is all-
embracing, nature is all-encompassing, and man's response must
be as a self-affirmed, self-assertive being in order for the process
of actualization to set in.

In this framework, the glory and the burden of man is
his response to responsibility for the development of his own
potential. The evolutionary thrust built into the human condition making him conscious of his possibilities — rather than

a fleeting notion of sick despair — is the dynamic responsible for commitment and for lifting us to the highest level of conceptualization and self-authentication. The overriding motive for commitment in personalism is grounded in a positive affirmation of life which stresses the gradual unfolding of the spirit and is based upon man's limitless potentialities for self-fulfillment.

III

1. ISAAC BEN SOLOMON ISRAELI

EVALUATION

Philosophy as Self-Knowledge

Isaac Israeli defines philosophy as a discipline concerned with the pursuit of self-knowledge. Man's unique position in the cosmos, combining both the spiritual and corporeal phases of life, projects human personality as the key to an understanding of ultimate reality. Forming an epitome of the universe, man, in knowing himself, knows everything. But a full knowledge of reality must involve us in a creative task instead of mere academic speculation. It should lead us to a knowledge of purposes and ultimate concerns in reality, especially to an understanding of the purpose of the union in man of body and soul. Whoever knows this purpose can realize what is truth and attain intellectual excellence and spiritual perfection.[1]

Isaac Israeli was a contemporary of Saadia. He was born in Egypt in 855, and was highly regarded as a physician. He later went to Kairuan where he served as court physician to several of the Fatimide Caliphs.[2]

He wrote at least five treatises on medicine which were translated into Latin and were studied by physicians in the European universities. In a small handbook, *Guide for the Physicians,* he stressed the moral aspects of medicine. A doctor, he maintained, must regard his work as auxiliary to the work of nature. "The physician does not bring about the cure, but he prepares the way for nature, nature is the actual healer." He also urged his fellow professionals to devote some time to heal the poor who could not afford to pay.

His philosophical works include the following: *The Book of Definitions* (*Sefer Gebulei Hadebarim*) which is extant in medieval Hebrew and Latin translations.

A fragment of the Arabic original was discovered by H. Hirschfeld among the Genizah manuscripts preserved in the Cambridge University Library and published by him in *J.Q.R.* XV (1902). The Hebrew translation was by Nissim B. Salomon and edited by Hirschfeld in the *Festschrift zum achtzigsten Geburstag Moritz Steinschneider, Leipzig,* 1896. The Latin translation was made by Gerard of Cremona, 1114 and edited by J. T. Muckle in the *Archives d'historie doctrinaire et litteraire du moyen age,* 1937-8, pp. 299ff.

The Book of Elements (*Sefer ha-Yesodot*) was translated by Abraham B. Chasdai and was edited on the basis of a Leyden manuscript by S. Fried, *Das Buch uber die Elemente,* Frankfurt, a.M., 1900. The Latin translation was by Gerard of Cremona, published in *Omnia Opera Ysaac,* Lyons, 1515.

The Book of Spirit and Soul (*Sefer ha-Ruah veha-Nefesh*) is available only in the Hebrew version, except for a short passage in the original Arabic. It was edited by Steinschneider, *Ha-Karmel* I, (1871-72), 202.

Commentary to Sefer Yezirah was reworked by his disciple, Dunash ibn Tamim. Fragments of *The Book of Substances* are extant in an Arabic manuscript and were first mentioned by A. Neubauer in the Second Firkovitch Collection of Hebrew and Judeo-Arabic manuscripts, *Oxford University Gazette,* 7, 1876-7.

As to Israeli's sources, and the background of his philosophical formulations, the biographical sketches have no clues to offer. Even the autobiographical reference in his *Book of Definitions* focuses only on the fact that he was a native of Egypt and that he lived there in 905, when he was about fifty years old. It is not clear, however, whether he spent the formative years of his life, prior to age fifty, in Egypt where he received his background in neoplatonic philosophy, or he studied in Baghdad and came under the influence of kalamistic thinkers? As with most medieval philosophers, then, we have to fall back primarily on internal evidence of the writings of the philosopher.

Extensive researches have been undertaken by several scholars concentrating on the main sources of Israeli's philosophy. The first is Solomon Fried, who edited Abraham B. Chasdai's Hebrew translation of Israeli's *Das Buch über die Elemente* in 1910, and gave us the first biographical sketch of Israeli, embracing his life, his works and sources, as well as his influence on later Jewish philosophers.

The second is Jacob Guttmann's *Die Philosophischen Lehren des Isaak ben Solomon Israeli* (Munster, 1911), which is considered the basic work on the subject and accepted completely by the historians of Jewish philosophy.[3] On the basis of a thorough analysis of all the editions of Israeli's philosophical works, Guttmann concludes that the neoplatonic theory of the universe — the doctrine of emanation — is the central thesis of Israeli's philosophy connecting all other concepts, which often appear disjointed, within the dominating neoplatonic framework. An important neoplatonic influence upon him was *Liber de Causis* attributed to Proclus from which he derived his theory of emanation. It is also apparent that he was acquainted with the works of Galen and Hippocrates as well as Democritus and Kalam. The atomistic theories of the latter he refuted by proving that geometrical points which by definition have location but not size cannot be put together to form a line. By the same token, discontinuous atoms, he argued, cannot be the source of continuous substance.

The other comprehensive work is *Isaac Israeli* by A. Altmann and S. M. Stern, Oxford University Press, 1958. The scope of their presentation is broad, embracing translations with comments and an outline of his philosophy. The major thrust of the authors is also to discover the sources for the salient concepts of Israeli's philosophy. The conclusion they reached is that Israeli is indebted primarily to Al Kindi and the Alexandrian commentators on the *Isagogue* for his philosophic formulations. A comparative study of both texts, Israeli's *Book of Definitions* and Al Kindi's philosophical treatises by M. Abu Rida, *Rasa'il al-Kindi al-Falasafiyya* (Cairo, 1950-3) with regard to the four types of inquiry, the definition of philosophy, the intellect, the soul, *creatio ex nihilo,* reveal Al Kindi's influence.

There is no doubt that their detailed source analysis has yielded new insight into Israeli's cultural antecedents. But does this study with its critical comments supply a coherent frame, a leitmotif, that offers a connecting link to the scattered features of his philosophic formulation. Moreover, it might be useful to find out something about Al Kindi and ask ourselves also about the sources of his philosophy. T. J. deBoer's article "Al Kindi" in the *Encyclopedia of Islam* refers to him as the first great Islamic philosopher.[4] who lived in the 9th century and was born in the city of Basra probably in 813 and died in 873. He studied in Baghdad and according to Munk (*Mélanges,*

340) and Steinschneider (*Al Farabi*, p. 7), he was considered
the foremost commentator on Aristotle. It is significant that his
relation with his Islamic contemporaries was completely negative. Their biographies rarely mention him. He was even sub-
jected to persecution by the Arabs. This has led many scholars
to doubt that he was a Mohammedan. There has even been
speculation that he was a Jew. *D'Herbelot's Bibliotheque
Orientale* (p. 278), asserted that he was a Jew, his name being
Abu Yusof Yakub Ben Ishak Al Kindi. Wolf (*Bibl. Hebr.* 3
ns 30, 1054b), moreover, speaks of him as a rabbi. So does
de Rossi (*Dizionario Storico*, p. 30, 55). Gesenius ("Arabische
Literatur" in Ersch and Gruber),[5] anxious to prove that the
astrology prevalent among Arabs and medieval Christians was
of Jewish origin, shared the opinion that he was a Jew. His
treatises defending the Unity of God and denying all positive
attributes to God, as well as his doctrine of absolute free-will,
the nature of the soul and intellect enhanced this view among
scholars.

Henry Malter in his essay "Al Kindi," *H.U.C.A.* Cincinnati,
1904, argues against this view. Flugel in his scholarly biography
"Al Kindi" (*Abhandlungen fur die Kunde des Morgenlandes*,
Leipzig, 1859), also refutes the supposition that he was a Jew.
Steinschneider (*Al Farabi*, p. 142) asserted, likewise, that
Al Kindi believed in the Koran, inasmuch as in his treatise on
astrology "On the Dominion of the Arabs and Its Duration,"
he indicates, by signs suggested in the Koran, the ultimate
victory of Islam over all religions and empires.

In either case, however, it is important to take note of Al
Kindi's sources. Scholars agree that the source for Al Kindi
was Plotinus (204-270) — who derived his neoplatonic construct ultimately from Philo (30 BCE — 40 CE) (Elmer

O'Brien, *The Essential Plotinus,* p. 15). The notion of the One, the Ego in *the Enneads,* goes back to Philo who effected a minor revolution in Greek thought that established as a point of departure in philosophy not sense nature but instead a wholly transcendent and unknowable One.

This brings us to the notion that the abiding temptations among historical scholars of ideas to account for every doctrine in a given author as an appropriation from someone who went before him really provides little clarification or critical evaluation of the author's claims and mode of discourse. What is crucial in any attempt at an analysis of a philosopher is the interpretation and the establishment of a leitmotif for the philosophical materials initiated or compiled by the author from sources that were already widely extant before the philosophers time. A critical analysis of a philosopher should concern itself primarily with what the philosopher did with the various doctrines which he derived often from diverse sources, in the formulation of a coherent central thesis consistent with the tradition of his school. The danger of contradiction often arises when an author accumulates knowledge and facts from a variety of sources without relating them to a distinctive worldview of his own.

Admittedly, what was extant at the time of Israeli and later medieval philosophers was an Aristotelian system as modified by neo-platonism. That system was supreme in its sway and frequently philosophers combined Aristotelian logic, physics and psychology with neo-platonic metaphysics. In the main, it is our contention, a Jewish philosopher had in mind a specific conceptual framework which dominated his worldview and every attempt to incorporate concepts and categories from other schemes of thought was meant to validate his central

thesis. Israeli was the first dialectic medieval Jewish philosopher
to formulate such a methodology. While he compiled his definitions and notions from a variety of sources, as pointed out
by Fried, Guttmann, Altmann and Stern — and the discovery
of precise sources undeniably constitutes scholarly achievements — the crucial issue in the evaluation of a Jewish philosopher is to discover the central thesis that made his mode of
discourse Jewish.

The personalistic framework seems to have been the
major concern of Israeli. Epistemologically, he describes philosophy as self-knowledge.[6] By knowing himself, man knows all,
"as in man are joined the ten categories of spiritual and corporeal substance and accident". Ontologically, Israeli describes
philosophy as a striving of man to imitate the divine by actualizing his potential.[7] This is accomplished by "understanding the
truth of things from their four natural causes, the material, the
formal, the efficient and the final cause" (*op. cit.*, p. 133).

The Aristotelian naturalistic explanation of the elements
in the sublunar realm as the direct creation of God, in contrast
to the neoplatonic emanationist explanation of the celestial
spheres, is central to his personalistic thesis of projecting the
uniqueness of man in the sublunar universe.

A basic discrepancy appears in Israeli's philosophy. In
the *Book of Definitions* the doctrine of emanation is developed
with great clarity concerning the supra-terrestrial sphere. God
created the Intellect, the Splendor. From it a spark of light
emanated and it became the rational soul. In due course
various divisions of the soul emerged. The sphere of the
heavens proceeded from the vegetative soul and as it thickened
it became visible. Here suddenly the scheme of emanation

comes to a close and we shift to a physical explanation of the universe in the *Book of Elements*. Since the nature of the sphere is to be a mover, the outermost sphere moves its neighbor and fire results. Air is derived from fire; water from air; earth from water. The combination of the elements in various proportions produces the vegetable, mineral, animal realms of experience. Thus, in his *Book of Elements* no reference is made to the doctrine of emanation. Terrestrial bodies are outside the process of emanation and the reason for that is that Israeli was fundamentally concerned with the nature and destiny of man in the sublunar universe. Man possesses a divine spark, a rational soul which like the Intellect, the cosmic hypostasis, was created directly by God and requires no intermediate successive radiations in this sphere. While essences descend one from another in a necessary sequence, and none could exist without the one preceding it, in an emanationist scheme, man's rational soul, is in a state of potentiality until activated by conscious efforts and intellectual excellence.

When actualized, the soul ascends to the level of the world of Intelligence, of Splendor, of supernal Wisdom. Manifestly, as regards the developmental process of man's rational faculty, the scheme of emanation with its successive radiations from the main source of light to the material and physical senses is not applicable either.

Moreover, as regards the physical dimension of man, in keeping with the Aristotelian doctrine of the elements, Israeli analyzes the number and character of the elements leading up to the composition of the human body. In this sense, the *Sefer ha-Yesodot*, although an exposition of the Aristotelian doctrine of the elements, is not primarily concerned with the problems of physics. It is rather a prelude to a study of the material nature of man and, as such, is linked to the personalistic notion reflected in his *Sefer Gebulie Hadbarim.*

His notion of the union of soul and body as the dimension of the spiritual final cause is central to the personalist focus on the primacy of man as a point of departure for all inquiry. Such a union combines the finite (the body) and the infinite (the actualized soul) by positing a reality that is experienced in anticipation, in transcendence.

By the same token, Israeli's personalist notion of man as a microcosm, makes no distinction between the human intellect and soul and the hypostatized universal Intellect and World Soul. Just as the universal Intellect (the species of things) has ever immediate knowledge, on the basis of the Aristotelian principle that pure thought is not separated from its object, so the human intellect comprehends by identification.

Central to personalism is his notion of immortality as rising above the sphere where the imperfect "revolve with the revolution of the sphere," symbolizing man's freedom from the natural forces of space and time and ascending to the timelessness and spacelessness of "the world of truth and apprehending the light of Intellect" (*Book of Definitions,* p. 132).

Likewise, his concept of prophecy is grounded in the notion of human development, and central in his notion of creation is that creation is for human reward.

It is, indeed, significant that Wolfson selected Israeli's psychology[8] — ("Isaac Israeli on the Internal Senses," *Jewish Studies in Memory of George A. Kohut,* edited by Salo W. Baron and Alexander Marx, New York, 1935) for his delineation of the first Jewish dialectic philosopher. Apparently,

Wolfson held that the major contribution of Israeli's philosophy was in the area of the development of the human condition.

The impact of Israeli's works among Jews, Christians and Muslims was considerable. Because of the popularity of his medical works,[9] his treatises on philosophy enjoyed a wide reputation among Christian scholastics and he was often referred to as the Jewish philosopher second only to Maimonides.[10] *The Book of Definitions* was translated into Latin as *Liber de Definicionibus* (1114) and the *Book of Elements* as *Liber de Elements*,[11] by Gerard of Cremona. These works were, thus, made available to the Latin schoolmen like Albertus Magnus, Thomas Aquinas and others[12] in the thirteenth century.

A Moslem work written in eleventh century Spain, *Ghayat al Hakim* makes reference to Israeli's philosophy.

The impact of Israeli's philosophical works on Jewish scholars is, indeed, significant. While Maimonides, in a letter to Samuel ibn Tibbon deprecates Israeli as a philosopher because of his neoplatonic orientation, other[13] Jewish philosophers speak with great admiration of his philosophy, despite the rising tide of Aristotelianism. Saadia corresponded with Israeli, according to the testimony of his pupil Dunash ibn Tamim.[14] It is also assumed that Saadia's doctrine of "rational laws" was to have originated with the Israeli concept of intellectual precepts[15] (*Book of Definitions*, on the description of philosophy). The Neoplatonic elements in Joseph ibn Zaddik's *Olam Katan* and in Solomon ibn Gabirol's *Mekor Hayyim*, as well as in the latter's reference to the four types of inquiry, suggest Israeli's influence. Moses ibn Ezra refers to the *Book of Definitions* and to a lost treatise of the philosopher. Abraham ibn Ezra quotes him in his commentary on *Genesis* 1:20 and 2:19. S. Fried in his introduction to *Sefer ha-Yesodot*

(*Das Buch Uber die Elemente*) collected the passages of various
Jewish philosophers in which Israeli is quoted. Some of the
post-Maimonidean philosophers who quoted Israeli include
Hillel B. Shmuel, Shem Tob Falaquera, Salomo B. Abraham
B. Aderet and Gerson B. Salomo. It should be noted that the
celebrated Bible commentator, David Kimhi, asked Abraham
ibn Chasdai, the translator of Al-Ghazali's *Balance of Action*
to translate into Hebrew Israeli's *Book of the Elements*, a request he complied with. In his preface to the Hebrew translation, Chasdai comments upon the profound appeal of Israeli's
philosophy.

Admittedly, it was not the neoplatonic orientation that
made the impact upon subsequent philosophers, many of whom
were Aristotelian. By the same token, the neoplatonic framework could not serve as a central thesis linking diverse concepts
that appeared on the surface as disjointed and unconnected.
No wonder Jacob Guttmann in his emphasis on Israeli's neo-
platonism as the core around which his philosophical mode of
discourse is organized wrote: "Israeli provides no biblical,
Talmudic or Midrashic documentation for his thesis — nor does
he supply proof for the existence of God or provide a rational
basis for the theological problems (*Die philosophischen Lehren
des Isaak ben Salomon Israeli*, Munster, 1911, p. 32). This
opinion is shared by other historians who argue also that it
does not appear that Israeli has written his treatises with the
avowed purpose of presenting a Jewish mode of thought.
Apparently, what we need to project is not simply a body of
conclusions based on an account for every doctrine as an
appropriation from another source, but a central, all-illuminating
scheme of thought which constitutes its organized principle of
life. What may have appeared as a collection of metaphysical

notions, often disorganized and unmotivated, takes on a coherent form relating to a central core. He appropriated what he believed to be best in the philosophical thoughts of other systems and adapted them to the requirements of his own scheme for the purpose of clarification and elucidation.

Accordingly, it was Israeli's definition of philosophy as primarily personalistic and his emphasis on man's participating role in orienting the self by transcendence and intellectual and moral self-realization that places him in the forefront of Jewish philosophic tradition. By positing the primacy of man as his leitmotif, the ideological construct of Israeli's philosophy reflects his avowed purpose of serving Judaism.

What follows is my translation of the first part of *Israeli's* work *The Book of Definitions*. He begins by formulating the four types of inquiry, the goal and the purposes of philosophic knowledge and concludes with his personalistic definition of philosophy.

SEFER GEBULEI HADEBARIM

The Book of Definitions

Isaac says: Many who observe the variations in the books of the ancients regarding the definition of things believe that this is due to differences in their opinion. This is not so. It is only when they attempted to explore the definitions of things that they discovered that there are four[16] distinct inquiries without which one cannot apprehend these definitions. The first is existence—when one inquires what this is. The third is quality—when one when one inquiries what this is. The third is quality—when one asks how this or that is. The fourth is purpose—when one inquires why this or that is.

Let me elucidate. With reference to existence, the inquiry centers on the existence of an object, namely, whether it exists or not. The answer this question provokes is either 'yes' if it exists and 'no' if one denies it. Essence investigates the nature or substance of a thing, namely what it is. The answer depends on the definition of the thing which reflects its nature and substantiality. Quality examines the attributes and the accompanying qualities of a thing recognizable through its existence. Hence before replying one should tell the inquirer that since an object has many attributes and concomitants, he should specify which one he has in mind. When he complies, we are in a position to answer either 'yes' or 'no' as we did before. Accordingly, the answer concerning existence is invariably 'yes' or 'no'. Purpose investigates the final cause of a thing which is necessary for the generation of an existent object, why it is so.

The following are some examples. If someone inquires whether man exists, the answer must always be "yes," because man has reality and what has reality has being, and what has being has necessarily existence. If someone inquires what is man, the answer is rendered by its definition, namely, that man is a rational mortal living being. "Living being" denotes his genus and his corporeality constituting the substratum for his form. Rationality and mortality are the differentiae completing his kind, as man alone is rational and mortal. If one asks how is man, the answer denotes quality which investigates the attributes and its extentions. Now, man's attributes are threefold. The first is that which is attached to every man at all times like laughter. The other is that which is attached to all men, but not at all times like grey hair when one grows old. Finally, there is a property attached to some men at some time like humility, medicine, scientific knowledge and similar things which constitute man's properties but are not attached to all new. Hence one must indicate which attribute he has in mind. When this has been clarified, one can answer 'yes' or 'no'.

If one inquires why man is rational, we may respond as follows: that he may discern things with his intelligence; investigate phenomena with deliberation and cogitation to establish the reality of things, and to do what is grounded in truth, justice and rectitude; pursue the good and shun evil in order that he may receive the reward of his Creator, may He be blessed.

When the philosophers established this notion and it became clear to them that definitions can be composed only from genera and substantial differentiae[17] but found for philosophy no genus from which its definition could be composed, they investigated, according to their sound judgment and understanding, and proceeded to describe it by three descriptions. One is derived from its name, another from its character and aim and a third in terms of knowledge.

The description derived from its name is that philosophy connotes love of wisdom. The term philosopher is of Greek origin. It is composed of *philio* and *sophia* and in Greek *philio* means lover and *sophia,* wisdom. It is clear, then, if philosopher means the lover of wisdom, philosophy is the love of wisdom.

The description in terms of its character and aim is the imitation of the Creator, according to man's capacity. This ideal of *imitatio dei* conveys the notion of imitating God's activities. By the words 'imitating God's activities' is meant the understanding of the reality of things which implies attaining true knowledge of them and doing what the truth requires. To know the truth of things is meant to understand them from their four natural causes which are the material, the formal, the efficient and the final cause.

The material cause is subdivided into its spiritual and corporeal aspects.[18] A case of a spiritual material cause is of the genera which are divided into their species and constitute the substratum for their forms which complete their kind, as, for example, 'living being' which is the genus of man and horse and other species, bearing their forms which establish their being. An instance of the corporeal material cause is silver which constitutes the matter for a ring and a coin and substratum for their forms, or gold which is the matter for earing and emeralds and substratum for their forms.

The formal cause is also of a spiritual and corporeal kind. A spiritual formal cause is like substantial forms predicated of the genus which constitute the essence of the species. The faculty of rationality applied to the living being constitutes the essence of man; the faculty of neighing which is also predicated of the living being species constitutes the essence of a horse. The corporeal formal cause is the material form of the human body and all other bodies.

The efficient cause combines likewise the spiritual and corporeal. An instance of the spiritual efficient cause is the power of the sphere, which the Almighty inbedded into the structure of nature rendering it impregnable against the effects common to the corporeal microcosm, such as generation and destruction, growth and decrease, health and disease, and other natural occurrences. A case of a corporeal efficient cause is the craft of the goldsmith fashioning a ring, the form of a picture painted on the wall, or the builder of a house.

The final cause is also either spiritual or corporeal. An example of a corporeal final cause is the form of a house and its completion which is necessary for habitation and proper protection, or the form of a ring in order that it should have a seal suitable for engraving. A case of the spiritual dimension of the final cause is the union of soul and body in order that the truths of the principles of science may become clear to man; that he may distinguish between good and evil, the desirable and objectionable, and that he may act in a fashion consistent with truth, justice and rectitude; that he may sanctify, praise and exalt the Creator and acknowledge His sovereignty; and desist from beastly, impure deeds, in order thereby to receive the reward from the Creator, which consists in cleaving to the upper soul and in the illumination by the light of intellect and by the beauty and splendour of wisdom. When one reaches this degree, he becomes spiritual as he cleaves to the light created by the power of God without mediator and will forever and in all eternity exalt and praise the Creator. This, then, is his paradise, the goodness of his reward, the bliss of his resting place, his perfect rank and untarnished beauty. In this sense, Plato speaks of philosophy as a zeal, a striving, a strengthening and the help of death. This is, indeed, a description of sublime meaning by the great philosopher. For in the expression 'the help of death,' he meant to indicate that philosophy helps to deaden all bestial lusts and pleasures. For in their mortification and deliverance from them one reaches the highest rank, the supernal splendor and will enter the realm of truth. But by indulging in animal lusts and desires until they become overpowering, he exposes himself to impulses that will lead him astray from his duties he owes to God, from pure fear of Him, and from prayer at the prescribed time.

This leads to another notion of which the philosophers speak and the intellect authenticates its truth.[19] He said that the Almighty has rational precepts which He vouchsafed unto his chosen among his creatures, namely, his prophetic messengers and the authentic sages who guide His creatures toward the truth and prescribe justice, recitude and the acceptance of things permissible; to pursue goodness, loving-kindness, humility and shun evil, injustice, theft, as well as refusing unlawful things. He, however, who does not embrace the rational commandments, which the Almighty has vouchsafed unto the chosen among His creatures, His priests, and teachers, but persists in his injustice, sinfulness, arrogance and corrupt ways, will be contaminated by his impurities and they will weigh him down and prevent him from ascending to the world of truth and from apprehending the light of intellect and the beauty of wisdom. He will remain confined beneath the sphere, mournful and in pain without measure revolving with the revolution of the sphere, in the intense fire and torturing flame. This will be his Gehenna (purgatory) and the fire of his torture, which the Almighty has reserved for the wicked and sinners who reject the precepts of the intellect.

Finally, philosophy is described in terms of knowledge. For philosophy is man's knowledge of himself. This is indeed a profound and sublimely intelligent description.[20] When a man attains a true knowledge of himself—his spiritual and corporeal aspects—he has knowledge of everything, viz. of the spiritual and corporeal substance. For in man are combined both substance and accident. Substance is twofold, spiritual and corporeal. The spiritual is like the soul and intellect; the corporeal, like the body with its dimensions of length, breadth and depth. Accident is, likewise, divided into the spiritual and corporeal. The spiritual is like humility, wisdom and other similar qualities perdicated of the soul. The corporeal accident are like the colors black, white, red, green and similar physical qualities predicated of the body.

Inasmuch, as man combines both elements, it is clear that when man knows himself in his spiritual and corporeal dimensions, he knows everything. He knows both the spiritual and corporeal substance and apprehends the first substance created from the power of the Creator without a mediator, which constitutes a substratum for diversity. He also knows the first generic accident which is divided into quantity, quality and relation, as well as the other six compound accidents derived from the composition of substance with the three simple accidents. When a man apprehends all these, he comprises the knowledge of everything and is worthy of being called a philosopher.[21]

ספר גבולי הדברים

חבור יצחק הרופא הישראלי
אשר העתיקו נסים בר שלמה רי"ת מלשון ערב ללשון הקדש
יוצא לאור על ידי
הצעיר נפתלי בן מו"ה אהרן הירשפעלד ז"ל

אמר יצחק רבים מרואי ספרי הקדמונים וחלוק דבורם בתכלית הדברים
זממו היות זה לחלוק סברתם בם והדבר אינו כן בעבור שנשתדלו לחקור על
תכליות הדברים מצאו להם שאלות ארבע שלא ישיגו לידיעת התכליות כי אם
בהן. האחת ההלות כאמרו הל מזה הוא או מזה והשנית המהות כאמרו מה הוא
זה והשלישית האיכות כאמרו איך הוא כזה או כזה והרביעית הלמות כאמרו
למה היה זה או זה. הפירוש כי ההלות חוקרת על הוית הדבר הנחקר הל לו
מציאות אם לא וכזה תפול התשובה בכל עת בהין אם המשיב יהיה מורה במציאות
או בלאו אם יהיה המשיב כופר לזה. והמהות חוקרת על טבע הדבר והוית
עצמו מהו ובזו תפול התשובה בתכלית הדבר הדורשת על טבעו והעצמות שלו.
והאיכות חוקרת על החזקות של דבר והדברים הרודפים אחריו בלי הפרד
ממנו הנכרים בעבור ההוייה באיזה מהם הוא לכן יצטרך המשיב שיחזיר השאלה
אל השואל לומר לו חזקותיו של דבר והרודפים אחריו רבים על מי אתה
שואל וכשיפרש הדבר בעינו לפי שהיה בסברתו ובחידתו ישיבו המשיב בהין
או בלאו כאמור למעלה ולכן בכל עת התשובה לא תפול בהלות ובאיכות כי אם
בהין או בלאו. והלמות חוקרת על העלה השלמית הצריכה למולד הוית הדבר
למה היה. ועל זה הראה אם יאמר השואל הל מאדם התשובה לא תפול בהלות
[ו]באיכות כי אם בהין או בלאו כי לכל אדם יש ברירות ומי שיש לו ברירות
יש לו הוייה ומי שיש לו הוייה מציאותו בהכרח בלי ספק, ואם יאמר השואל
ומה הוא האדם ישיבו המשיב בתכליתו לאמור האדם הוא החי המשכיל המת
כי החי מורה על סוגו והחומר שלו הנושא צורתו והשכל והמיתה הן פרקיו
ותשלום מינו שאין משכיל ומת כי אם האדם, ואם יאמר השואל ואיך היא האדם

משיב לו האיכות חוקרת על חזקותיו של דבר ורודפיו וחזקותיו של אדם
מתחלקות לשלשה הראשון כי יש דבר שמתחבר עם האדם כלו בכל זמן כמו
הצחוק ויש שמתחבר עם האדם בכלו אך לא בכל זמן כמו שיבת האדם בעת
זקנותו ויש שמתחבר בקצת האדם ובקצת הזמן כמו הענוה והרפואה וחכמת
המראה והדומה להם ממה שהוא מוחזק באדם אך לא בכולו אם כן תאמר לו
על מי מההחזקות ההם אתה שואל וכשיפרש השואל מה שרצה בשאלתו ובחידתו
משיבו המשיב בהין או בלאו ואם השואל למה היה האדם חי משכיל
אמתת הדברים ולעשות מה שהוא ראוי מה האמת מה הצדק והיושר לרדוף
אחרי הטוב ולהתרחק מהרע כדי שישיג גמול בזה מבוראו ית׳. ובעת עמוד
פילוסופים על זה המכון ונתברר להם כי התכליות אינם נרכבות כי אם מסוגים
ומפרקים עצמיים ולא מצאו לפילוסופיאה סוג שממנו תהיה נרכבת תכליתה
דקדקו לפי טובת תכונתם ומחשבתם וחקיקות משלש חקיקות האחת אצולה משמה
והשנית לקוחה מחזקתה והשלישית מחכמתה והחקיקה האצולה משמה היא
הפילוסופיא בפירוש היא אהבת החכמה וזה השם יוני הוא ומורכב מלשון יון
כי פילו הוא אהבה ושופיא היא החכמה ואם הפילוסופיא היא אהבת החכמה
והפילוסוף אוהב החכמה מזה נתברר פירושה. והחקיקה הלקוחה מחזקתה היא
כי הפילוסופיא נדמית לבורא ית׳ לפי כח האדם וסברת דברי נדמית לבורא
נדמית לפעולות הבורא וסברת דברי נדמית לפעולות הבורא היא שעומדת על
אמתות הענינים היא בבירור ידיעתם לעשות מה שצריך האמת. וסברת דברי
שעומדת על אמיתית הענינים היא שעומדת עליהם מארבע העלות הטבעיות,
שהן העלה החמרית והצורית והפעלת והשלמית והעלה החמרית יש רוחנית
ויש גשמנית והרוחנית כמו הסוגים המתחלקים למיניהם ונושאים לצורתם
ומשלימים למינותם כמו החי שהיא סוג האדם והסוס וכל מיניהם והוא נושא
לצורותם המקימות הוייתם והעלה החמרית הגשמית היא כמו הכסף שהוא
חמר הטבעת והמטבע והנושא לצורותם וכמו הזהב שהוא חמר הנזם והרביד ונושא
לצורותם. והעלה הצורית יש רוחנית ויש גשמנית והרוחנית כמו הצורות העצמיות
הנשואות על הסוג בהקמת הוויית המין כמו השכל האנושי על החי בהקמת הוית
האנושי והצהל על החי בהקמת הוית הסוס, והצורית הגשמית כצורת הגשם כגוף
האדם וגוף כל דבר. והעלה הפועלת יש רוחנית ויש גשמנית והרוחנית כמו כח
הגלגל אשר תיקנו האל בטבע ומדדו בו מתואר כל מה שיש בעולם הצעיר
הגושמנית מנולד והספד מגידול וכלייה ומבריאות וחלי ומהדומים להם פעלי

הטבע והעלה הפועלת הגושמנית כמו מלאכת הצורף בטבעת וצורת התבנית
המצוייר בקיר ופועל הבונה בבית. והעלה השלמית יש רוחנית ויש גשמנית והעלה
השלמית הגושמנית בצורתן[ן] ושלימותו הצריכה לשוכני הבית ההיא כדי לעמוד
בה בלי פחד וצורת הטבעת להיותה מפותחת כדי לחתום בה והעלה הרוחנית
כמו קשר הנפש בגוף כדי שיתבררו לאדם אמתות עניני החכמה להבדיל בין
טוב ובין רע והדברים הנחמדים לדברים שאינם נחמדים לעשות מה שהוא
ראוי מהאמת מהצדק ומהיושר לקדש הבורא ולשבחו ולהללו ולתן הודייה
למלכותו להתרחק מהמעשים הבהמים הטמאים להשיג בזה גמול בוראו ית'
והוא שיתדבק בנפש העליונית לקבל אורה מאור הדיעה ויופי החכמה ומזוהרה
וכשיגע אל זו המדרגה יעשה רוחני בהדבקו באור הנברא מעוז אל נורא בלי
בינוני ויעשה מהלל משבח לבורא מעולמי עד וזהו גן עדנו וטובת גמולו ונעם
מנוחתו ומעלתו השלם ויופי התמים ולכן אמר אפלטון כי הפילוסופיא היא
זריזות והשתדלות והתאמצות ועזרת המות. אמר יצחק כי זה החכם הגדול הרחוק
מהעול העולה בסברתו רצה במאמרו עזרת המות עזרה היא להמית כל התאוות
הבהמיות ותענוגיהן כי במיתתן ובההצלה מהן תהיה המעלה היתרה והזהר
העליוני להכנס בבית האמת ובהחיות התאוות והתענוגים הבהמים ובהתחזקם
ינתן ביד מי שיתענו מחובת חקי האל ומיראתו הטהורה ומהתפלה תמיד
בזמניה הכתובים וזה מורה על דבר אחר שאמרו הפילוסף והדיעה תעיר
לצדקו באמרו ולאל יש מצוות דיעניות יראיהן על בחירי ברואיו רצה בזה
על נביאיו השלוחים ועל חכמי הצדק והאמת המנהיגים ברואיו אל האמת
המצווים בצדק וביושר וקבול העניינים מהתר לרדוף אחר הטוב והחסד והענוה
ולהתרחק מהרע והמעול ומהגזלנות שלא לקבל ענין הבא מאסור ומי שאינו
מתדבק במצות הדיעניות שהראן האל על בחירי ברואיו וכהניו וחכמיו ומתמיד
בעולו ובחטאתו וגסותו וברוע מעלליו יטמאוהו חטאיו בטמאתם ויצורו עליו
ובכבד שלהם יכבד ולא יוכל לעלות אל העולם האמתי ולא ישיג בנר הדיעה
וביופי החכמה וישאר במצר תחת הגלגל אבל כואב בלי חק מתגלגל בגלגל
הגלגל באש האביר החזק ובלהבה המיסדת וזהו גהינם שלו ואש יסודו שהכינו
האל לרשעים ולהחטאים החולקים על מצות הדיעה. וחקיקת הפילוסופיא מחכמתה
היא כי הפילוסופיא היא הכרת האדם נפשו וזו עוד חקיקת הרחוק מהעול העולה
בדעתו כי האדם כשיכיר נפשו בהכרה אמתית ברוחניותיה וגשמניותיה מחזיק
בהכרת הכל ר"ל בהכרת העצם הרוחני והעצם הגושמני כי באדם מתקבצים
העצם והמקרה והעצם שני עצמים רוחני וגושמני והרוחני הוא כמו הנפש

והדיעה והגושמני הוא כמו הגוף הארוך הרחב העמוק וכן המקרה יתחלק לרוחני
וגושמני והרוחני כמו הענוה והחכמה כל הדומה להם במקרים הרוחנים הנשואים
על הנפש והגושמני כמו השחור והלבן ואתרוג ואדום והירוק והמקרים האחרים
הגושמנים הנשואים על הגוף. ובהיות זה בזה, נתברר כי האדם כשיכיר נפשו
ברוחניותיה וגושמניותיה תחזיק בהכרת הכל והכרת העצם הרוחני והעצם
הגושמני ומכיר העצם הראשון הנברא מעוז הבורא בלי בינוני המוחזק במשא
החלוף. ומכיר המקרה הראשון הסוגי המתפרד אל הכמות והאיכות והסמיכות
ומכיר שאר המקרים הששה המורכבים הנולדים מהרכבת העצם עם המקרים
השלשה הפשוטים וכשיחזיק האדם באלו כולם או מחזיק בהכרת הכל וראוי הוא
להקראות שמו פילוסוף.

2. BAHYA IBN PAKUDA

THE "MINOR" TREATISE SEFER TOROT HA-NEFESH

A Personalistic Response to the Mechanistic Naturalists

EVALUATION

In 1896, Isaac Broydé published a Hebrew translation[1] of
a treatise "On the Essence of the Soul," written originally in
Arabic under the title *Kitab Ma'ani al-Nafs*. Despite its neo-
Platonic structure, Dr. Broydé attributed the work to Bahya ibn
Pakuda, author of *Hovot Halevavot* which is Kalamistic in
content and opposes the notion of creation as a graded series
of emanations. Other scholars, however, beginning with Jacob
Guttmann[2] and followed by Goldziher,[3] maintain that the author
of *Sefer Torot ha-Nefesh*, although a contemporary of Bahya
was someone other than he and they refer to him as pseudo-
Bahya. They support their claim by at least two arguments.
First, they contend, there is an apparent discrepancy in the two
works relating to the sources of the doctrine of creation and
unity. As we mentioned, the author of *Torot ha-Nefesh* seems
to be under the influence of neo-Platonism, while Bahya follows the Kalam. The second argument points to the avowed
opposition by the author of *Torot ha-Nefesh* to the Mutazila on
the ground that they are followers of the naturalists whose notions are not in accord with the Bible and the authentic philosophers.

I am inclined to agree with Isaac Broydé especially in view
of a Parsee[4] manuscript discovered in the early nineteen twenties,

ascribing the treatise to Bahya ibn Pakuda. The first argument
advanced by the scholars disputing the authorship of Bahya of
this text cannot be taken too seriously. For one thing, the lines
between neo-Platonism and Mutakallimum were not drawn that
sharply among the medieval philosophers after the tenth century.
Neo-Platonism served largely as a religious scheme rather than
as a metaphysical system. As such, it was introduced into Islamic
literature by the *Ihwan al-Safa* (Brethren of Purity) and its
doctrine of emanation was used in a somewhat loose and popul-
lar form as Islamic neo-Platonism. Surely by the time this text
appeared, the doctrine of creation was combined with that of
emanation to such a point that distinctive differences between
the two concepts had been erased.

Accordingly, we find, as I pointed out previously,[5]
that Isaac Israeli likewise employed both doctrines interchange-
ably. In his *Book of Definitions,* he used the notion of emanation
and in his treatise "On the Elements," the doctrine of creation.
Apparently, the major concern for the medieval Jewish philosopher was not so much to establish the nature of the origin of the
world as that of man's soul being created directly by God, endowing the human species with a measure of sovereignty. Which-
ever scheme served to underscore the spiritual essence of the soul
as a creation of the Divine Will and Wisdom was embraced by
the philosophers. Accordingly, Isaac Israeli applied one cosmological framework to the celestial sphere and another to the
sublunar. By the same token, it was possible for Bahya to make
use of both concepts in his two works as long as each doctrine
helped to establish the hierarchical level of creation.

The other argument levelled against a common authorship
for both works is based on the forthright opposition to the Mutazila by the writer of *Sefer Torot ha-Nefesh.* But this assump-

tion is easily refutable, when we keep in mind that there were two Mutazila sects—the Basra and the Baghdad Mutazila—and that the author's opposition was aimed at the former sect. It is, indeed, amazing that the critics of Broydé were not aware of this historical fact. The Basra sect, to which the author of *Torot ha-Nefesh* makes reference, was under the influence of al-Djubbal and his son Abu Hashim who promulgated a more naturalistic philosophy than the Baghdad group with respect to Divine control over human action and the relation of the soul to the body. Our author's opposition to the al-Djubbal sect of the Mutazila was therefore no indication of a total rejection of the Mutakallimum. It was the naturalism of the al-Djubbal that he repudiated, and there is no justification to allude to the author of *Torot ha-Nefesh* as anti-Kalamist.

This brings us to the crucial issue that coalesces both treatises, namely, the onslaught against a naturalistic secularism and mechanism by means of personalism. It is only a personalistic scheme projecting subjective man in a state of self-confrontation, who can affirm the reality of a dimension which transcends the phenomenal world. As a contemporary theologian[6] has pointed out that when we examine man we find a strange contradiction. He appears to be a part of nature, partaking of her ways, subject to her laws, but at the same time he has the capacity to stand aside, to behold, to transcend and to control nature for his own creative purposes. He is the only being who participates in nature and yet, by his ability to behold it, differs from it radically. He is the only phenomenon who appears to be outside the immutable patterns of the natural world as known by science. And although scientific naturalism may argue that any deviation from the uniformity of nature is only a seeming exception which more advanced scientific investigation will disprove, yet when it comes to an examination of the nature of man, naturalistic empiricism is inadequate. For here the very act of self-awareness, when man confronts and recognizes himself as part of nature is already an indication that he is also a free spirit beyond the natural data.

By the same token, Bahya in *Sefer ha-Nefesh* defines philosophy as "man's self-knowledge"[7] which has an organic character of its own and stands in opposition to a naturalism, which fails to take into account the realm of the spirit where the self exists in an undefined, developmental situation. Man's spirit is not an accident of the body nor a defined primary substance but a transcending self-subsistent entity, surmounting claims to absolute universality of physical law. Similarly, in his *Hovot Halevavot*,[8] he affirms that from the *olam katan* — the microcosm, the human species which is the ultimate purpose of the existence of the larger world — we derive evidence of Divine wisdom and design in all Creation. He states:

> When we have arrived at an understanding of the matters noted in regard to man much of the mystery of the universe will become clear to us, since the one resembles the other. And, thus, some sages declared that philosophy is man's knowledge of himself, that is, knowledge of what has been mentioned in regard to the human being so that through the evidence of Divine wisdom displayed in himself, he will become cognizant of the Creator; as Job said (Job 19:26), "From my flesh, I behold God."

Manifestly, by projecting human personality as a primary datum, the personalist makes two assumptions. One, that the self as a spiritual nature transcends the level of a physical, biological organism and thrusts us into another realm of the spirit. Secondly, it formulates a body of propositions making claims about reality in existential terms eluding fixed mechanistic properties, and positing the realizable end and ultimate concerns

as absolute, and the cohesive integrated whole as real.

What follows is my translation of the first chapter of *Sefer Torot ha-Nefesh* embodying two principles of a philosophy of personalism.

SEFER TOROT HA-NEFESH

It is proper for you to know that knowledge of the soul is related to knowledge of the Creator of the soul, may His name be exalted, and its mysteries, subtleties and ramifications. It is possible that you have already delved into many books on this topic and considered different views and various theories on the matter of the soul. One of the philosophers, however, has said already that "philosophy is man's knowledge of his soul"; furthermore, whoever knows his soul better knows his Master better.[9]

Pursuing diligently this matter, I determined, with the help of the Creator, may His memory be exalted, after considering and reflecting upon all other schemes that this (personalistic view) is the authentic world view and correct doctrine, grounded in logical and speculative proof and upholding our religious heritage and tradition without apologetics or contradictory claims. It is, moreover, independent of any other scheme and pursues its own organic character out of love for the truth and a disposition for righteousness, endowing man with superiority as stated in Scriptures, "the way of truth have I chosen"[10] . . . "And snatch not the word of truth out of my mouth, for I wait for thy ordinance."[11]

Examining the essential doctrines of the externalists, I noted that they are divided into two opposing groups. One group consists of the naturalists and the other of the metaphysicians. I perceived, further, that most of the notions of the true philosophers are derived from our Torah and its commentaries; while the thought modes of the naturalists contradicts Scripture and are at variance with the insights of the metaphysicians.

Subsequently, I inquired into the statutes and modes of thought as delineated in our sacred Torah and discovered that our concepts relating to the soul are in most cases compatible with those of the true philosophers. On the other hand, I noted that not a single scriptural insight nor most of its narratives are in accord with the naturalists, with the exception of the following two sects. One is a sect of an Islamic school called the Mutazila,[12] which was related to Abu Hashim al-Djubbal,[13] author of a dialectical theory of modes[14] and identified by the name al-Djubbal because of the nature of this sect. The other group of Jewish origin is referred to as the Karaites.[15]

Now, the doctrine of the naturalists is that the soul is a corporeal property and an accident borne by the body and when the latter disintegrates and disappears, its property and accident dissolve with it. There is, accordingly, no immortality of the soul after the destruction of the physical organism that bears it. This is the view of one group of the Mutazilites and the Karaites who maintain that, inasmuch, as the soul is an accident of the body, that when the latter is corrupted its accident shares the same fate.

To be sure, those of the Mutazilites who believe in the hereafter hold that at the time of the resurrection, God will bring the parts of the body together with its accident, the soul, and will reward or punish them. But there is no point in discussing the nature of the soul in relation to the problem of resurrection, as we are presently not involved in the question of resurrection. Know this!

The opinion of the Bible and the true philosophers is that the soul is a spiritual substance, existing prior to the body and continuing to exist after its dissolution. As a self-subsistent entity it can never happen that the soul disappears even if the body ceases to exist.

Now, I found a third doctrine which maintains that the soul comes into existence together with the body but does not disintegrate with the cessation of the body. This is the view of Ibn Sina[16] (Avicenna) and it does not coincide with the Bible and the authentic philosophers who hold that the soul must be prior to the object it is attached to, as the senses precede the object of sense and the intellect the object of apprehension.

I noted, however, that in his work *al-Mabda wa-al Maad* (*The Beginning and the Return*), Ibn Sina deduced from the Koran the assertion that the soul originates with God and returns to God. This obviously is in agreement with our Scriptures. He writes: "Alas, thy silent soul, return to your Master that thou desirest!" This is similar to Solomon's observation, "And the spirit returneth unto the Lord who gave it."[17] Ibn Sina's further statement to the effect, "that the return of the soul will be to the place whence it came," is another indication of his agreement with the Biblical view of the world to come. His own observation, however, with reference to the creation of the soul with the creation of the body, which he alludes to in the previously mentioned work, does not conform to Biblical doctrine. Know this![18]

ספר תורות הנפש

לרבנו בחיי בן יוסף הדיין הספרדי
(בעל „חובות הלבבות")

פרק ראשון

ראוי לך לדעת שידיעת הנפש תתיחס לידיעת בורא הנפש יתעלה שמו
ולמסתריה ודקותה ורוב ענפיה. ויוכל היות כי כבר הגית בספרים רבים
בזה הסעיף והתבוננת אל דעות שונות ושיטות מתחלפות בענין הנפש וכבר
אמר אחד מן החכמים „הפילסופיא היא ידיעת האדם את נפשו" ונאמר ג״כ מי
מכם היודע יותר את נפשו יודע יותר את רבו. ושקדתי בזה עד שעזרני היוצר
יתרומם זכרו כי בריתי לי מכל זה מה שעלה על דעתי שזאת היא הדעה
האמיתית והשיטה הנאמנת מכל אשר עמדתי עליו המתאמת עם השכל והחקירה
והעוזרת להקבלה והמסורה בלי נשיאת פנים ותחרות ואיננה מתיחסת לשום
שיטה אלא תאהב את האמת ותלך בעקבותיה ותפנה אל הצדק ותן לו היתרון
כמה שנאמר דרך אמונה בחרתי וגו' ואל תצל מפי דבר אמת כי למשפטיך
יחלתי.

הנה ראיתי כי ראשי שיטות החצוניות נחלקים לשתי מפלגות המתנגדות
זו לזו מפלגת האנשים הנקראים בעלי הטבע ומפלגת האנשים הנקראים בעלי
האלהות. וראיתי כי רוב דברי בעלי האלהות אשר הצדק אתם נגזרו מן התורה
ונלקחו מן פרשותיה וראיתי כי רוב דברי בעלי הטבע מתנגדים להתורה
וישתנו ממה שהזכירו בעלי האלהות אחרי כן ראיתי רוב דברי החקים והתורות
ומצאתי כי דעתם בענין הנפש תתאחד על הרוב עם דעת בעלי האלהות
הנזכרת בתורה הקדושה וראיתי כי אין אחת מן התורות עם רוב מספרן תתאחד
עם דעת בעלי הטבע חוץ משתי מחלקות מחלקה מן המוסלמאנים הנקראת
„אלמעתזלה" המתיחשת לאבי האשם „אבן אלגבאי" רצוני לומר מחבר חכמת
הדבור והנודעת בשם „אלגבאיין" על מחלקתם ומחלקה אחת מן היהודים הנודעת
בשם „הקראית".

ודעת בעלי הטבע היא שהנפש עדי גופני ומצב מקרי הגשוי על ידי
חמר הגוף וכשכלה הגוף ונאבד חמרו כלה עדיו ונאבדו מקריו עמו ואין לעולם
השארה להנפש אחרי הריסת נושאה וכן הוא דעת חלק אחד מהמחלקה
המעתזלה וכל המחלקה הקראית כי הם חושבים שהנפש היא מקרה וכאשר יאבד
הגוף יאבדו מקריו עמו ואלה מהם אשר יאמינו בעולם הבא אמרו כי יוי׳ ישיב
בעת תחית המתים חלקי גוף האדם אל המקרה אשר הוא נפשו ויגמלהו או
יענשהו ואין ענין לדבור הנפש ומצביה עם עניני תחית המתים כי אין אנחנו
מתעסקים בתחית המתים דע זה.

ודעת התורה ובעלי האלהות אשר הצדק אתם היא שהנפש עצם רוחני
ההוה קודם הגוף והנשאר אחר כלותו ולא יתכן לעולם שתאבד הנפש אף אם
יאבד הגוף. ומצאתי דעה שלישית והיא שהנפש מתחדשת בהתחדשות הגוף
ולא תכלה בכלות הגוף וזה דעת אבן סינא ואיננה מסכמת עם התורה ולא עם
דעת בעלי האלהות אשר הצדק אתם מפני שהנפש קודמת לדבר אשר יקשר
אליה כמו שהחוש קודם לדברים המוחשים והשכל קודם לדברים המושכלים.
וראיתי מה שהזכיר אבן סינא בספרו ״הנפש והעולם הבא״ ראשית מאמרו
מתאחד עם תורתנו והוכיח מתורתו שהנפש תרד מן יוי׳ ותשוב אלא יוי׳
הוא יאמר: ״אהה את הנפש השוקטת שובי אל אדוניך אשר רצית בו״ וזה
דומה למה שאמר שלמה ע״ה והרוח תשוב אל האלהים אשר נתנה. ואבן סינא
יאמד עוד ״וההשבה לא תהיה אלא אל המקום אשר ממנו באה״ והמאמר הזה
יתאחד עם מה שאמרה התורה מן העולם הבא אבל מאמרו בהתחדשות הנפש
עם התחדשות הגוף אשר הביא בספרו הנזכר לא יתאחד עם התורה. דע זה.

3. ABRAHAM BAR HIYYA

A Comprehensive Personalism

EVALUATION

Abraham bar Hiyya is the first comprehensive personalist philosopher firmly rooted in biblical and rabbinical tradition. In his two philosophical works, *Hegyon ha-Nefesh* and *Megillat ha-Megalleh,* he gave full sway to every aspect of the personalistic scheme of thought.

Epistemologically, like his predecessor Isaac Israeli and his contemporaries Bahya ibn Pakuda and Moses and Abraham ibn Ezra, he maintained that philosophy is self-knowledge. By knowing himself, man knows all. Quoting from Job (19:26) "From my flesh, I shall behold God," Bar Hiyya asserts, "from the shape of your body and the structure of your organs you can comprehend the wisdom of your Creator." He further states: "I maintain that philosophers commenced their investigation by considering the form of man and demonstrated that he is the ultimate of created things because we find in him additional combination and composition over and above that found in other creatures. For the definition of man which conveys his essence, is the rational animal. "Animal" in this definition refers to the body which grows, develops and eventually perishes. 'Rational' refers to the faculty of reasoning logically, to distinguish between good and evil and to recognize wisdom and reason" (*Heg. ha-Nefesh,* p. 2). In *Megillat ha-*

Megalleh (3, p. 60), he likewise asserts: "When Scripture has completed the account of the creation of man, it begins to re-interpret cosmology and metaphysics is a new form and in a different perspective."

Moreover, the reality of things is apprehended as an epistemological monism. On the basis of the Aristotelian principle that pure thought (form and species of things) is not separated from its object, Abraham bar Hiyya also asserted that the human intellect comprehends by identification. For to him, wisdom (*hakhmah*) is identified with the soul of man. *Ki hakhmat ha-adam hi ha-nefesh* (*Heg. ha-Nefesh*, p. 17). What the mind postulates and acquires is accorded objectivity. "Any potential object which wisdom affirms its realization must have already changed to actuality" (*ibid.*, p. 5).[1] Since the ultimate in man's nature is the acquisition of wisdom, the latter constitutes the standard of truth verification.

Accordingly, personalism is the key to knowledge, inas-much as in an existential framework, the only knowledge worth having is knowledge that bears directly upon human experi-ence. If reason is identified with the soul of man, then the authentication of man's soul endows reason with an ontological content as an inner idealized order corresponding to the natural order of the universe. While in the initial stage, the truths of reason are true by definition, like mathematical axioms, reason in the ultimate stage assumes a new epistemological orienta-tion, denoting "the life of reason," that is reason widened beyond bondage to exclusively empirical scientific experiences. Bar Hiyya uses two terms *nefesh ha-hogeh* and *nefesh ha-hakhmah* to distinguish between the two modes of reason, dis-cursive reasoning and the content of knowledge as a realizable entity.

Ontologically, personality is an existence in suspense. Authentic existence is something constantly to be won. Personalism constitutes a metaphysics of "not-yet," a state of becoming, a state of dialectic, a reality that is experienced in anticipation, in transcendence. *Hashibat-ha-adam,* the absoluteness of self, oriented by self-transcendence constitutes the central core of the Hebraic scheme. Personalism projects a new concept of being in terms of functional substantialism and activity instead of static substantiality. In conscious self-existence and self-experience, there is a mark of reality in which unity co-exists with multiplicity, identity with change, the empirical with the transcendent. Bar Hiyya grounds his personalistic scheme on two fundamental categories. First, *Kabbalat ha-Torah,* the revelatory process which is projected as the initial stage for man's development from a state of potentiality to actuality and secondly, *Yihud ha-Shem,* God's Unity which projects our self-conscious drive directing our pure unified concepts toward a purposeful end of identifying cognitively with God's wisdom and eternity. Man's authentic existence is consummated as he moves from *Kabbalat ha-Torah* to *Yihud ha-Shem.*

Methodologically, man is the frame of reference in philosophic speculation. We start with a consideration of human personality. The point of departure for all inquiry is an investigation into the nature and destiny of man.

A crucial problem of philosophic inquiry, in any religiously-oriented scheme of thought, is the legitimacy of such an enterprise that often begins with doubt. Conceivably, any religious philosophy runs counter to the very essence of the philosophical pursuit, which dictates that its concepts proceed with no binding antecedent convictions, no unquestioning presuppositions, no undeviating affirmations. For is not a religionist committed to the doctrine of faith prior to embarking upon philosophic inquiry? By definition he cannot engage in any make-believe that such a faith is not ultimately normative for his thought. He can only theologize, which means he can only proceed from the supernaturally achieved truths of faith or, at best, engage in a mode of philosophizing (provided you define philosophy as a free way of thinking about any discipline) employed to render clearer the word of God, which is the only source from which the theologian can draw his claims. But the classical notion of philosophy is to find the principle of things as they could be grasped by the natural structure of the human mind, projecting formal philosophical truths defined in terms of its content. Bar Hiyya addresses himself to this question in the opening remarks of his philosophical treatise *Hegyon ha-Nefesh*. He states that "This biblical reference ('From my flesh, I shall behold God' (Job 19, 26), gives us permission to investigate the views of the classical philosophers and their theories of creation" (p. 2). Thus, in making the idea of personalism basal and interpreting reality in personal terms, we have initiated an area of investigation wherein we may inquire without preconceived assumptions and presuppositions into the nature and destiny of man. As Bar Hiyya has pointed out, we may legitimately begin our philosophic investigation by probing an apparent contradiction in scriptures regarding the nature of man. One biblical verse crowns man with honor and glory, exclaiming, "Thou hast given him dominion over the works of Thy hands, everything hast thou placed beneath his feet" (Ps. 8, 7); while the other tends to demean his stature, stating, "how much less the mortal, the mere worm, and the son of earth the mere maggot" (Job 25, 6). What, then, is man in the Hebraic perspective? Is he an exalted being endowed with consummate perfection or a lowly creature born with irremediable inadequacies and unregenerative depravity? What is his relation to nature and ultimate reality? Is creative activity to be ascribed to him? Does personality, moreover, imply self-consciousness? Does it imply freedom? What about man's destiny? Is he to be regarded as the goal and final cause of the world? Is man immortal?

These are some basic questions about which there may be legitimate differences of opinion paving the way for an authentic philosophical exploration. Preoccupation with man's unique role in the cosmic scheme reflect such questions of fundamental importance that they serve to underscore our deepest metaphysical quest for knowledge in ultimate reality interpreted in personal terms.[2]

Bar Hiyya, thus, points specifically to personalism as the leitmotif for the philosophic methodology of the Hebraic scheme. By positing the dialectic condition of man as portrayed in the Bible, we are necessarily involved in an intricate full-scale line of inquiry concerning some of the basic insights of the philosophical pursuit. Once we focus the rationale of a Jewish ideological construct on man, there is room enough for an independent discipline to exercise analytic judgments for validating its claim. Personalism, according to Bar Hiyya, projects a methodology which permits us to philosophize without preconceived notions and, as such, can be defined in terms of its own achieved truths, leading to a knowledge of the universe and God's existence and unity — *metziat ha-Boreh* and *Ahdut ha-Boreh*. Our existential situation will draw us into the unfoldment of ultimate truth, beholding the Transcendent from man's perspective in a two-fold aspect, God-in-Essence and God-in-Relation. Quoting from Isaiah (57, 15),

'*Thus saith the High* and Lofty One who dwelleth forever, whose name is holy' Bar Hiyya asserts that "Height' (*Rom*) is an absolute attribute of God—God-in-Himself, while 'Loftines' (*Nisa*) is a relative term denoting the position of God in relation to man and the world (*Heg. ha-Nefesh*, p. 9).[3] Accordingly, the oft-quoted admonition by the rabbis of the Talmud not to engage in esoteric speculation regarding matters "above and beneath the heavens; before and after creation" (T.B. Hagigah 11b), does not include the pursuit of investigating the nature and destiny of man, which necessarily points to a Transcendent beyond ourselves.

Ethically,[4] in the realm of human behavior, Bar Hiyya goes one step further in his methodology. Inasmuch as ethical judgments are of a practical nature, Bar Hiyya maintains that they may be reducible to the concepts of natural science. Ethical theory may be regarded as naturalistic for the simple reason that the goals of human behavior are always related to means. There is a moral law in the nature of things corresponding to the natural law. Hate is an aberration of the physical laws of nature as well as the moral judgment of the spirit. It is only when man's true rational nature develops to the fullest, that we can apprehend the naturalistic aspects of ethical theory. By the same token, in contemporary society, the elimination of war in a nuclear age is not only a moral imperative; it is a natural law which has to do with man's primary urge of self-preservation.

Accordingly, Bar Hiyya asserts: "We maintain that the Ten Commandments, heard by all the Israelites at Mt. Sinai, embraced both aspects of the Almighty's voice. In the beginning the Israelites heard the voice of admonition implying a state of choice of acceptance and a willingness to be guided by its precepts. Admittedly, the meaning of "Thou shalt have no other gods before me" and the other commandments that follow was in the nature of an injunction and an admonition in this voluntaristic manner persisting from the time of Revelation to the Final Redemption. Thus there were some among them who were receptive to the voice of God and acted properly; others did not. Some were meritorious; others, transgressors. The intention of the Almighty, blessed be His name, however, was to infuse ultimately the commandments with instinctual, involuntaristic fulfilment, so that the injunction, "Thou shalt have no other gods before me" would leave us no choice but remain forever an utter impossibility. Beginning with the Messianic period the people of Israel will be compelled to accept the Torah in a proper fashion. They will not have the possibility or choice to stray from the Torah, just as all phenomena of creation possess no choice to deviate from the irrevocable laws built into their very structure. Thus all Israelites in the days to come will conduct themselves like the consecrated saints whose conduct we described at the outset of our discussion."

Historically, Abraham bar Hiyya was the first Jewish philosopher to expound a philosophy of history. In his *Megillat ha-Megalleh,* he attempts to find a religious explanation of the whole process of history by establishing an exact correspondence between world eras and the days of creation.[5] There is, thus, a divine plan of history and the series of periods would find their realization in the messianic age.

Additionally, the overriding significance of Abraham bar Hiyya's works on the structural level — apart from his comprehensive conceptual personalist contribution — lies in the fact that he developed his philosophy in clear interaction with biblical and rabbinic sources. Firmly rooted in the religious tradition of Judaism, he espoused a personalistic philosophy as the point of departure for his methodology, epistemology, ontology and ethics. In his pursuit of giving biblical and rabbinic interpretations of philosophic views, Abraham bar Hiyya retained his individuality and could not be pigeonholed as an appendage to neoplatonism as most historians of Jewish philosophy maintained. To be sure, he adopted the fundamental concepts of Aristotle and other Aristotelian notions colored by neoplatonism, as pointed out in my work *Judaism As a Philosophy: The Philosophy of Abraham bar Hiyya*. But once he projected a central affirmation which became its organized principle around which revolved all other thought forms including those incorporated from other systems, the organic character of his discourse was self-determining and developed creatively from within. Thought modes appropriated from other schemes, instead of weakening the distinctive character of the Hebraic world-view, enhanced its claims by elucidating its insights and rendering them more clear, more consistent, and more fully developed with respect to their implications. It is only when we accumulate knowledge and facts without relating them to a central thesis and a distinct methodology that necessarily follows from it, that the danger of contradiction and apologetics arises.

Bar Hiyya demonstrated his independent philosophical mind in three ways. First, by grounding general philosophic notions in biblical sources. Consider his exposition on the Aristotelian concepts of matter and form. He writes: "There are the ideas of the ancient sages, and we shall find that they are drawn from the Torah. Thus matter and form are indicated in the second verse of Genesis, 'And the earth was *without form* (Heb. *Tohu*) and *void* (Heb. *Bohu*).' *Tohu* is matter; *Bohu* signifies that through which matter gains existence, hence form. "Water" (Heb. *Mayim*) is also a general word for any of the various forms, whereas "light" (Heb. *Or*) stands for the pure subsistent form. By "firmament" (Heb. *Rakia*) is meant the second kind of form which unites with the pure matter in a permanent and unchangeable manner. 'Let there be a *firmament* in the midst of the *waters*' (Gen. 1, 6) indicates that the "firmament" is embraced by the bright light of the first day, that is the universal form, from which all the other forms come. 'And let it divide between *water* and *water*' (ibid.) signifies that the "firmament" stands between the self-subsistent form and the third kind of form above mentioned, namely, that which unites with body and gives rise to substances changing their forms, like minerals and plants. The "luminaries" (Heb. *Meorot*) correspond to the second light mentioned above. We shall find also that the order of creation as given in Genesis coincides with the account given above in the name of the ancient sages."

In *Meg. ha-Meg.* (p. 22) he identifies the various intelligible substances with manifestations of divine light which correspond to various biblical theophanies, the world of the angels and seraphim and the word of the souls in future bliss.

A second approach that marked Bar Hiyya's originality was to reinterpret general philosophic views in rabbinic terms. This is especially the case with reference to his cosmogony where he discusses at length the various kinds of form[6] and matter as expounded by the "wise men of other nations and, subsequently, proceeds to reinterpret them in a rabbinic and midrashic orientation. Consider, for instance, his exposition on the four categories in which form can exist in the celestial and terrestrial bodies, which he describes first in philosophical terms and recasts later in rabbinic terminology. In philosophic terms, he describes the division first, as self-subsistent Form which never combines with matter, such as all the forms in the upper world. Second, Form that is attached firmly and inseparably to matter, such as the form of the firmament and the stars. This form can never change. Third, Form attached to matter temporarily, but moving from body to body and changing shape, namely the bodies of terrestrial beings. These two forms, which are joined to matter, have not the power to separate from matter and exist apart from it as they had done originally. Finally, there is one more part which can logically exist, and this is form which is attached to a body, but is eventually separated from it and returns to its pristine condition to exist on its own without matter. 'Matter' here is what we originally called '*Tohu*' but now referred to as 'creature' or 'created thing.' This remaining division is, according to the philosophers, the human soul. Reason and logic force us to admit that there exists a created form which clothes matter, and after its creation merits separation from matter becoming self-subsistent as originally. And we find no Form deserving this, other than the human soul. Bar Hiyya then proceeds to delineate the division in rabbinic termonology as follows: Those worthy of permanence in this world and the world to come; those that are permanent in this world, but not in the world to come; those that are permanent neither in this world nor in the world to come; those that have no permanence in this world but are permanent in the world to come. No fifth category is conceivable. We will, therefore, examine these four categories in the creation story and through them we can learn the nature of all things.

Finally, if there appears a irreconcilable conflict between

certain notions of the speculative philosophers and the Hebraic tradition, he asserts his independent approach and rejects the speculative in favor of what seems to him to be the biblical approach. Consider the case of theodicy which prompted a variety of theories among speculative philosophers. There is the theory of the dualists espousing two separate and supreme powers: One, the Creator of the good and the other of evil. This view obviously undermines the very essence of a monotheistic faith.

Abraham bar Hiyya lists two other solutions which he also finds untenable. There is the view that evil is a conditional property, contingent upon the refusal of the sinful to repent, while good is unconditional and absolute. Such a theory, however, is inadmissible for it creates a schism in the Almighty's scheme of creation. Moreover, the good is also conditional upon the endurance of the righteous in their righteousness.

Another view offered by many philosophers and drawn from Platonic sources is that evil is a negative property. It is the absence of good, just as blindness is the absence of vision, deafness the absence of hearing and darkness the absence of light. This understanding of evil as a negative property does not mean that evil is an illusion and can be disregarded It implies rather that it is not created by God directly. God produces the positive, the good forms, and determines them to last a definite span of time. When this time comes to an end, the forms disappear and pain and evil take their place just as darkness comes when light goes out.

Abraham Bar Hiyya, however, did not accept this solution, for it ran counter to biblical thought. There is ample evidence in Scripture that God is the cause of evil as well as good, and this is the meaning of the word "judgment" (Heb. *Mishpat*) that occurs so often in the Bible in connection with God's attributes. The same idea is expressed in Jeremiah (9, 23) "I am the Lord who exercises loving kindness, (*hesed*), charity (*tzedakah*), and justice (*mishpat*) in the earth." Loving-kindness refers to the creation of the world, which was an act of pure grace on the part of God, since the actualization of the potential was not necessary *per se* but based on God's loving-kindness. Charity refers to the rewards accorded the righteous in the world-to-come, which is an act of charity for the majority of these people. Justice denotes the good and evil distributed in this world according to the law of justice. Thus, God is the author of both good and evil in this world. Although, He exercises loving-kindness and charity in the world to come, in this world He reigns with justice. For in this world God's omnipotence is so central that we can limit His goodness. However, the affliction of the righteous in this world is not meant as a punishment, but rather as in the case of Job a test of moral strength, which is followed by a double measure of reward in the hereafter. The wicked, on the other hand, are punished for their evil deeds in this world, so that they may have a share in the hereafter, unless their wickedness is irredeemable—in which case they are endowed with riches and prosperity in this world in order that they may have no claim on the next world.

Abraham bar Hiyya was born in Soria, Spain in 1065. As a member of the Zerubbabel family, he occupied a high position at one of the Moslem Courts. He was held in high esteem by several rulers on account of his astronomical knowledge. Together with his contemporary, Abraham Ibn Ezra, he was a disciple of R. Moshe ha-Darshan, who as a teacher was noted for his vast erudition in talmudic and worldly culture.   Bar Hiyya, however, surpassed his Jewish contemporaries in scientific knowledge as is evidenced by the fact that he assisted other scholars in their translation of scientific works and some of his own writings, such as the fifth chapter of *Megillat ha-Megalleh,* which was translated into Latin and French and widely used as source material on the astronomy of his day. In addition, he stood preeminent as the first scholar to write original philosophic and scientific works in Hebrew. His works are quoted profusely by his successors especially Maimonides who referred to him as "one of the most brilliant minds of Spain." His writing is lucid and simple in language and style.

What follows is my translation of a portion of the first chapter and the last portion of the fourth chapter of *Hegyon ha-Nefesh.* The translations reveal Bar Hiyya's remarkable contribution to every dimension of the personalistic scheme as well as a fresh approach to the concepts of Messianism and *Olam Haba.*

SEFER HEGYON ha-NEFESH

CHAPTER I

Abraham bar Hiyya, the Spharadi said: Blessed be the Lord, the God of Israel, Master of all creatures, Great in counsel and Mighty in performance, Who instructs man in wisdom and skills and has endowed him with a capacity to have dominion over all the inhabitants of the transient world, as it is written, "Thou hast made him rule over the works of Thy hands; everything hast thou placed beneath his feet" (Psalms 8:7). Elsewhere, however, Scripture states, "How much less the mortal, the mere worm and son of the earth, the mere maggot?" (Job. 25:6).

It is, therefore, incumbent upon every intelligent person endowed with reason and judgment to inquire and to investigate the unique and superior quality of mortal man — although but worm and maggot and likened unto vanity — that makes him worthy of having control and dominion over all beasts and cattle and gives him the capacity to rise to the highest degree of reason and wisdom.

We have found that most of the ancient wise men of other nations, who were inclined to examine religious questions, although they were not privileged by the Almighty to share in the knowledge of our sacred and authentic tradition, explored this subject matter in accordance with their wisdom and conception and discovered that the correct method to arrive at an understanding of things as they are was to examine the origin and principles from which all existing things have been created. From a knowledge of a thing's basis and origin, its construction and function can be understood. For every building is composed of its constituent stones by which it is identified. Once a person comprehends their arrangement and their number he will understand how it is built and can reconstruct it exactly as it was without adding or subtracting anything from it.

Scripture alludes to this when it says: "Know therefore this day, and reflect in thy heart, that the Lord is God in the heavens above and upon the earth beneath; there is none else" (Deut.

4:30). If you understand thoroughly the nature of the heavens above and the earth beneath, you will at once acknowledge and comprehend that God made it in his wisdom, and that He is the only one and there is no one beside Him. The book of Job, in like manner, observes "And from my flesh, I shall behold God" (19:26). This signifies that from the form of the body and the structure of its organs, we can see and understand the wisdom of the Creator. This Scriptural reference gives us permission to investigate the views of the ancients and their theories about the nature of existence.

It is my contention that the wise men started their investigation from a consideration of the form of man and demonstrated that he was the ultimate of created things because we find in him additional combination and composition over and above that found in other creatures. For the definition of man which conveys his essence is the "rational animal." (*haiha-dabron*). "Animal" mentioned in this definition, refers to the body which grows and develops organically and moves and eventually ceases to be and perishes. "Rational" (dabron) does not refer to the faculty of speech but to the power of reason, of inferring one thing from another, of discriminating between good and evil, of identifying every discipline. It is reason that distinguishes man from all animals. This is conveyed in the definition by the term rational, whereas the other aspects are included in the definition common to animals.

We find that the definition of a plant is a body that sprouts and grows and in the end withers but does not move or possess motion. This is simpler than the definition of animals which have the additional power of motion and movement by which they are distinguished from the plant kingdom. And if we further inquire into the definition of stones, metals, seas, rivers, hills, valleys and other inanimate bodies on the earth, we shall discover that generically they are bodies that can change their forms and shapes, but they have no power to increase in size and growth. Plants are therefore distinguished from them by their power of growth and increase in size.

The general principle that evolves from this is that bodies

whose form can be changed but have no capacity to increase in size are the simplest of all bodies on earth. If you compare them to the heavenly bodies you will find that the form of the earthly bodies is changeable and temporary, whereas the form of the heavenly bodies is permanent—although the term is applied in either case and the elements of the definition are similar in both.

We find, further, that body which is common to all created things can be defined as breadth, depth and length attached to something that has magnitude. Upon deeper reflection of this definition, we find that body is composed of two elements which theoretically are originally distinct and separate, and existed before in (God's) Pure Thought only potentially until His Will joined them together. Ancient philosophers refer to one of them in Greek as "hyle" (matter), implying that it has no likeness or form but has the capacity of receiving likeness and form. The second element they call form describing it as that which has the power to clothe the hyle with likeness and form. The hyle is too weak to sustain itself and to free its deficiencies unless form attaches itself to it. Form, on the other hand, is not perceived or sensed unless it clothes matter which bears it. It is obvious, then, that each of them needs the other and is designed to help it to exist or to be perceptible to beings of the world. Without the form, the hyle could not exist and without the hyle, the form could not be perceived. The form, however, is superior to hyle, because it needs hyle only to be perceived and seen but can exist by itself without being seen; whereas the hyle would not exist in any manner without the aid of the form. This is the explanation in terms of their relationship.

Moreover, each one of them is divided further into two parts. The two parts of the hyle are the pure, clean part and the dregs and sediment. The two parts of the form are the closed and sealed form, too pure and holy to be attached to hyle and combined with it, and the second part which is the open and penetrable form fit to be linked with the hyle and be contained in it. The splendour of the self-subsistent form, which is too pure to be combined with the hyle, gazes and illuminates the penetrable form, enabling it to clothe the hyle with all forms which the hyle is capable of receiving.

Now, these two principles, namely, hyle and Form were lodged before God and existed potentially until such a time as He saw fit to produce them. 'Time' is used here as a figure of speech and according to human usage. In fact, however, before things moved from a state of potentiality to actuality there was no Time. When all things were potential, so was time for time has no substance and is only a measure signifying the duration of existing things.[7] Without such existing things there is no measure on which time depends.

They say, that when Pure Thought (God) determined to actualize them, He strengthened the pure Form to come into existence and to be clothed with its splendor, which no hyle can touch. This Form, which is not attached to the hyle, is the Form of angels, seraphim, souls and all forms of the upper world. Not all men can see or conceive in the mind these forms as they are not attached to anything visible and the majority of people cannot comprehend a thing not perceptible to corporeal senses. The essence of these forms can be understood only by the profoundly wise, capable of scientific investigation. In fact, this Form remained in its position with the light shining inside it. Its light then emanated upon that form which was fit to unite with the hyle and strengthened by the word of God and His command to combine with the hyle. First, it was joined to the pure clear matter and this was a firm attachment that will never change as long as they are joined. From this combination the heavenly bodies were created. Subsequently, the Form united with impure hyle, giving rise to all kinds of bodies in the sublunar world which change their forms but do not change their position such as the four elements—earth, water, air and fire —and the products of their composition as far as vegetation and plants.

Now, we find that all their ideas and words that we have explained so far, are derived from the Torah and drawn from our source of Wisdom. Upon reflection we find that the hyle and the Form which, according to them, existed potentially before creation are the *Tohu* and *Bohu* referred to in the Torah. Indeed, this is what the world consisted of prior to being realized *in actu* at the word of God, as we read: "The earth was *Tohu* and *Bohu*

(Gen. 1, 2). If you compare the explanation of the term "hyle" given by the philosophers as that which has no shape or form and cannot exist on its own with the meaning of *Tohu,* you will find them to be identical. For *Tohu* is that which has no magnitude, no sensation, no substance, or utility as the Torah says: "After *Tohu* which cannot profit or deliver, for they are *Tohu*" (I Samuel 12, 21). This indicates that they have not the power to help themselves or others because they are *Tohu,* having no existence, shape, and form. It is further written: "Not for *Tohu* (naught) did he create it, to be inhabited did he form it" (Isaiah 45, 18), inferring that *Tohu* has no existence and permanence. Thus, whatever they said of hyle may be said about *Tohu.*

Form, they described, as that which has the power to clothe the hyle with shape and form. The term *Bohu,* because it is constructed from two words, *Bo* (in it) and *Hu* (it is), has a two-fold implication. The Bible states *Tohu* and *Bohu,* i.e., it has no sensation, no stability or anything else by which *Tohu* can exist except by *Bohu,* the form which covers the *Tohu* and sustains it. Proof of this can be derived from the verse: "He shall stretch over it the line of *Tohu* and the plummets of *Bohu* (Isaiah 34, 2). The line is useless for balancing the building unless it sustains the plummet which shows whether the building is straight or crooked. For this reason the Bible links it to *Tohu,* stating "the line of *Tohu.*" It links the plummet with *Bohu* because the plummet demonstrates whether the weight is straight or crooked, just as the form structures the shape of created things. The Bible says "line of *Tohu*" in the singular because the *Tohu,* which is devoid of sensation and permanence is unique and has not the power to separate and divide itself. But it says "plummets of *Bohu*" in the plural because the forms that clothe it appear in many shapes.

I repeat that the term *Bohu* is divided into two words, *Bo* and *Hu* because the clear, closed, pure form is self-subsistent, requiring no assistance. Hence the meaning of *Bo - Hu* is that which is self-subsisting and self-powered even without being linked to any other thing. This explanation of *Tohu* and *Bohu* is superior to the other explanations offered by the philosophers.[8]

SEFER HEGYON ha-NEFESH

CHAPTER IV

To explain its[9] true meaning,[10] we maintain, that the verb
shema "to hear" in the Hebrew language is used in our present
context in a three-fold manner. There is first the physical connotation of listening by ear, unrelated to the comprehension of the
subject matter, such as "I had only heard of thee by the hearing
of the ear" (Job 42:5), "And when Abraham heard that his
brother was taken captive" (Gen. 14:14). Secondly, the term
shema connotes obedience to someone's counsel or command as,
"And Jacob had obeyed his father and mother" (Gen. 28:7);
"And Abram heeded the voice of Sarai" (Gen. 16:3); "And
they will hearken unto thy voice" (Ex. 3:18); "Thou shalt not
consent unto him, nor shalt thou hearken unto him" (Deut. 13:9).
Finally, *shema* implies understanding as we find "speak we pray
thee unto thy servants in the Syrian language for we understand
it" (Is. 37:11); "that thou canst understand a dream to interpret it"
(Gen. 41:15), that is to say to apprehend its interpretation. Thus,
the verb "and hearkenest" in the verse "So that thou returnest
unto the Lord thy God and hearkenest unto his voice" (Deut. 30:2)
has the third connotation, which implies understanding and does
not convey acceptance as is its common usage.

Accordingly, when we are told that "the sound of the voice
you heard, but any similitude ye saw not save a voice" (Deut.
4:12), the implication is that the Israelites heard and accepted
the voice in its ordinary sense, but failed to see its image with
the heart's "eye" and comprehend the form of that voice and
its inner meaning except the audible sound, as the verse concludes "there was nothing but a sound."

The voice that emanates from the Omnipotent directed toward
the sublunar world possesses either one of two characteristics. It is
either in the form of a decree realizable simultaneously with the
Almighty's utterance such as the injunction "And God said, let
there be light" (Gen. 1:12), as well as the other divine utterances

by which the world came into being. Then, there is the other
aspect, the voice which admonishes and commands, which is not
instantly implemented as God said to Adam, "Of all the trees
of the garden thou mayest freely eat, but of the tree of knowledge,
of good and evil, thou shalt not eat of it" (Gen. 2:16-17).

We maintain, that the Ten Commandments heard by all the
Israelites at Mt. Sinai embraced both aspects of the Almighty's
"Voice." In the beginning the Israelites heard the voice of admonition, implying a state of choice of acceptance and a willingness to be guided by its precepts. Admittedly, the meaning of
"Thou shalt have no other gods before me" and the other commandments that follow was in the nature of an injunction and an
admonition in this voluntaristic manner, persisting from the time
of Revelation to the Final Redemption.[11] Thus, there were some
among them who were receptive to the voice of God and acted
properly; others did not. Some were meritorious; others, transgressors. The intention of the Almighty, blessed be His name,
however, was to infuse ultimately the commandments with instinctual, involuntaristic fulfillment, so that the injunction "Thou shalt
have no other gods before me" would leave us no choice but
remain forever an utter impossibility. Beginning with the Messianic
period the people of Israel will be compelled to accept the Torah
in a proper fashion. They will not have the possibility or choice
to stray from the Torah, just as all natural phenomena of creation
possess no choice to deviate from the irrevocable laws built into
their very structure. Thus, all Israelites in the days to come will
conduct themselves like the consecrated saints whose conduct we
described at the outset of our discussion.

Our scriptural text proceeds to elucidate clearly this matter
and its implications. Following the verses quoted above we read:
"And the Lord Thy God will circumcise thy heart and the heart
of thy seed to love the Lord thy God with all thy heart and with
all thy soul in order that thou mayest live" (Deut. 30:6). We
have here the promise that the Lord will remove the hard crust
and the foreskin that prevents us from comprehending the voice
of the Lord in its manifold aspects in order "that thou mayest live,"
in the world-to-come where there is eternal life.

Now, in a previous chapter we read "to love the Lord your God and to serve him with all your heart and with all your soul" (Deut. 11:13). The passage concludes by stating: "In order that your days may be multiplied and the days of your children in the land (*ibid.*, 21). The implication here is that when you are motivated to love God with all your heart and all your soul because of His commands, or because of conducting your affairs as a submission to His will, then the Almighty will cause you to prosper in this world, which because of man's sins has deteriorated from its original course intended for it at the time of creation, and made dependent for its prosperity and regeneration upon man's own spiritual transformation. However, when your love of God is derived involuntarily from the Almighty's immutable decree, the world will prosper automatically following its natural course for which it was created irrespective of man's action. Hence, there is left no other form of reward for man's labors except eternal life in the hereafter. That is why the concluding verse refers only to the exclusive reward of the world-to-come, "that thou mayest live" (*ibid.*, 30:6), whereas the preceding verses allude to man's reward in this world as we find: "that I will send rain for your land in due season" (*ibid.*, 11:14), and concludes with the words "In order that your days will be multiplied" (*ibid.*, 21).

You will discover this central theme in the prophecy of Jeremiah when he states: "Behold days are coming, saith the Lord, when I will make with the house of Israel and with the house of Judah a new covenant" (Jer. 31:31). The prophet refers to the days of redemption whose advent, we hope, will be speedily accomplished with God's mercy when all the exiles of Israel and Judea will be delivered. The prophecy continues: "Not like the covenant I made with their fathers on the day that I took hold of them by the hand to bring them out of the land of Egypt, inasmuch they have broken my covenant, although I was a lord over them, saith the Lord" (*ibid.*, 32). This is to say "they have broken my covenant," because I left the choice of the fear of heaven and the practice of good deeds in their own hands; "and I was a lord over them" implies that they did not fulfill my precepts properly.

The prophet then proceeds: "But this is the covenant that I will make with the house of Israel after those days," after the present exile. "I will place the law in their inward parts and upon their hearts will I write," that is to say, that instead of engraving the Law upon tablets of stone, as I did for their ancestors, I will inscribe it on the tablets of their hearts[12] to be enshrined forever, never to be forgotten. The prophet then concludes, "And I will be unto them a God and they shall be unto me a people. And they shall not teach any more every man his neighbor, and every man his brother saying, know the Lord, for they shall know me, from the least of them even unto their greatest, saith the Lord, for I will forgive their iniquity and their sin will I not remember any more" (ibid., 32-33).

You will find the implication of this comforting message in the promise that the Holy One will destroy the evil inclination and stamp it out from the world so that all will have faith in God from their childhood to old age. The Almighty will, moreover, forgive all former iniquities from the time of Adam onwards and improve man's heart that was evil from childhood.

The same theme is expounded by Ezekiel in a different version when he declares: "And I will give you a new heart, and a new spirit will I put within you, and I will remove the heart of stone out of your body and I will give you a heart of flesh. And my spirit will I put within you and I will cause that you shall walk in my statutes and my ordinances ye shall keep and do them" (Ez. 36:26-27). In the first verse the prophet makes reference to God's double endowment to men of "a new heart and a new spirit" which they possessed previously in a different manner and in another form. He then proceeds to describe the old heart beat which he will remove from their flesh as a heart of stone. Comp. "and I will remove the heart of stone out of your body" (ibid).

It is well now to inquire in what way the hearts of people in this world may be compared to stone. We know that every limb of the body when stimulated to perform its proper function requires no special training or guidance. It performs its function naturally for the specific purpose for which it was created.

We say, for instance, that God created feet for walking, the hand to grasp and lead, the ear to hear, the eye to see, the heart to understand and to reason. Every limb was created to be useful to man in a specific manner and does so whenever man so wills. Not a single limb requires training or repeated action for its prescribed task except the human "heart" (the mind) which cannot implement its specific assignment without prior guidance, instruction or training; and from that training it acquires a faculty or a spirit to understand, to guide itself as well as the other faculties of the body that depend upon it. Now, this spirit that it acquires may be either good or evil, and will determine the leanings of the heart, which will likewise turn out to be either good or bad. In this respect, then, the heart is likened unto a stone for the latter cannot move by itself from one place to another, nor change its form but depends upon man's will for its movement and the change of its form. Likewise, the heart has not the capacity to rule over its acquired spirit or alter its course but rather follows the dictates of the latter. This is unlike the other limbs of the body that require no external pressure, but are controlled and activated by the original potential with which they are endowed. This is why the prophet compares the heart to a stone for, indeed, in its present state, it must be referred to as a stone. However, when the Holy One, blessed be He, will remove from the heart the characteristics of a stone and endow it with the qualities of the other limbs of the body to control the faculties implanted in them, then He will allude to the heart with the appelation of "flesh," similar to the other limbs of the body, as it is written "and I will give you a heart of flesh" (*ibid.*).

Now, it is significant that the prophet does not describe for us the nature of the form of the old spirit that is being removed as a substitute for the new spirit, as He delineated previously the nature of the old heart which is referred to as a stone. The reason for that is because the spirit which the heart acquires in this world is not a self-existent entity at the time of its creation but something that enters from without and develops through constant training and habitual practice. Or to put it a different way, we might say that the spirit is a potential which may be actualized by habitual practices and constant development. At

the time of Redemption, the Holy One will act upon this spirit
in the hearts of His people which heretofore existed potentially
as a force for both good and evil and he will actualize it as an
exclusive force for good, as we read "and my spirit will I put
within you" meaning, my good and upright spirit. The heart will
then act upon this spirit in the same manner as the other limbs
without necessary recourse to special training as was the case
formerly.

It is further written: "And I will cause that you shall walk in
my statutes and my ordinances ye shall keep and do them" (*ibid.*).
This indicates that while the fear of God, the worship of his
name and righteous conduct were formerly only in a state of
potentiality, the Holy One will henceforth implant them uncon-
ditionally in the hearts of men, leaving them no choice for deviation.
At the Messianic era all the people of Israel as well as the
proselytes who will live at that time, as we derived from the
Scriptural verses interpreted before, will pursue one mode of
conduct with a sense of consecration and reverence. They will
implement automatically the precepts enshrined on the tablets
of their hearts and articulated orally and consequently all trans-
actions of this mundane world will be conducted in an equitable
fashion. Supporting evidence of this is apparent to any student
versed in Scriptures such as the verse "Love thy neighbor as
thyself" (Lev. 19:18). This precept will be practiced and ful-
filled by all inhabitants of the world at the time of redemption.
Moreover, when all people will love one another as themselves,
envy, hatred and greed, which are the cause of wars and strife in
the world, will disappear. That is why the prophet envisions the
Messianic era as a period when: "And they will beat their swords
into ploughshares and their spears into pruning hooks. Nation
will not lift up sword against nation" (Micah 4:3). The observance
of this precept alone protects us from five prohibitions that constitute the foundations for the other injunctions of the Torah
starting with the commandment "Thou shalt not kill" until the
end of the Decalogue.[13]

ספר הגיון הנפש
לר' אברהם בר' חייא

העמוד הראשון

פתיחת ההגיון בתשבחות לאל עליון

אמר אברהם בר חייא הספרדי, ברוך ה' אלהי ישראל אדון כל בריה,
גדול העצה ורב העלילה, המלמד לאדם חכמה ותושיה, והשליטו על כל יושבי
נשיה, כדכתיב (תהלים ח) תמשילהו במעשי ידיך כל שתה תחת רגליו, וכתוב
אחר אומר (איוב כ"ה) אף כי אנוש רמה ובן אדם תולעה. וחייב הוא כל איש
מבין אשר לו דעת ומזימה, לדרוש ולחקור באיזה מדה גדולה ועצומה, זכה
האדם אשר הוא תולעת ורימה, ולהבל דמה, להיות לו ממלכה וממשלה על כל
חיה ובהמה, ולהעלותו אל מעלת המדע והחכמה. ומצאנו רוב חכמי האומות
הקדמונים אשר היה להם חלק בתבונה, והכינו לבם לחקור על כל דרכי
האמונה, ואע"פ שלא זיכם המקום למעלת התורה הקדושה והנאמנה, חקרו על
הענין הזה כפי חכמתם וכפי השגת ידם, ומצאו הדרך הנכונה ללכת עליה
המוציאה אל מעמד העליון ומקומו בכל מסלוליה. היא החקירה על שרשי
הנמצאות, אשר ממנו היו נבראות. והעומד על יסוד הדבר וראשיתו, יכול
הוא להבין דרך מעשיהו וסדר תבניתו. כי כל בנין אשר הוא קשור ומחובר
אל אבניו אשר נתחבר מהן הוא נכר, והעומד על סדרן ומנינן, יכול הוא
להבין דרך בנינו לתקנו בדרך הראשון בלא תוספת ובלא חסרון. והכתוב
נתן רמז לענין הזה באומרו (דברים ד) וידעת היום והשבות אל לבבך כי ה' הוא
האלהים בשמים ממעל ועל הארץ מתחת אין עוד. אם אתה מבין בכל לבבך
סדר מעשי השמים אשר עליך והארץ אשר תחתיך, מיד אתה מודה ומבין כי
הבורא ברא אותו על חכמת תבניתו, ואחד הוא לבדו ואין אלוה מבלעדו. הוא
שאמר הכתוב (איוב יט) ומבשרי אחזה אלוה. מתבנית בשרך ותקון אבריך
אתה יכול לראות ולהבין חכמת בוראך. והרמז הזה מרשה אותנו לחקור על
דברי הקדמונים ואיך היו כל הנמצאות לפי דעתם.

ואני אומר כי החכמים ההם התחילו במחקרם מצורת האדם, ובאו להורות
כי הוא היה סוף הנבראות, מפני שמצאו בו החיבור והמרכבה מוספת על הנמצא
בכל בריה. כי גדר האדם המודיע את שרשי יצירתו, הוא החי הדברן [והחי]
הנזכר בגדר הזה, הוא הגוף הצומח והגדל מאליו, והוא הולך ומתגדל וסופו
להאסף ולהחדל. והדברן אינו נאמר בכאן על מלול הפה וצפצוף הלשון, כי אם
על הכח המדע להבין דבר מתוך דבר ולהפריש בין טוב לרע ולהכיר כל
מזימה וכל מדע ומדע, ובכל חכמה האדם נפרש מכל חיה ובהמה, והם נמצאים
בו מן שם הדברן אשר הוא נמצא בגדרו, ושאר החלקים הם נמצאים
בגדר בעלי חיים. ותמצא גדר צמח האדמה אשר הוא צומח מאליו וגדל וסופו
להחדל, ואינו יוצא ממקומו ולא מתגלגל, מופשט מגדר בעלי חיים. מפני שבעלי
החיים מוסיפים עליהם ההליכה והגילגול הנמצא בהם ובתוספת הזה נפרשים
מהן. ואם אתה חוקר על גדר האבנים והמתכות וגם ימים ונהרות והרים וגבעות,
ושאר הגופים אשר הם בארץ נמצאות, יהיה הגדר הכולל אותם שהן גופות
ממירות את צורתן ומחליפות את תבניתן, ואין בהן כח שיהיה מאליו מרבה
את שיעורו ולא מגדיל את גופן. ונמצא צמח האדמה מוסיף הרבוי והגידול
הנמצא בהן, והוא ההפרש אשר ביניהן. ויהיה הכלל העולה בידך שהגופות
הממירות את צורתן ואין כחן להוסיף על מדתן הן הגופות הפשוטות מכל אשר
בארץ. ואם אתה מקיש אותם אל גוף הרקיע תמצא ההפרש ביניהן שהצורה
הנמצאת באלו מתהפכת ונחלפת, וצורת הרקיע על תבנית אחת עומדת כל
הימים, ושם הגוף נאמר עליהם וחלקי גדרן נאמר בשתיהם. ותמצא גדר הגוף
הכולל את הנמצאות הוא רוחב ועומק ואורך שהוא נדבק אל דבר שיש לו
ערך. והמעיין בגדר הזה עיון יפה ימצאנו מחובר משני דברים, וראויים הם על
שיקול הדעת להיותם מקדם נפזרים ונפרדים, ולפני המחשבה הטהורה בכח
הם עומדים, עד בא רצונו להדביקם ולהחבירם. והחכמים הקדמונים קוראים
לאחד מהם בלשון יווני היולי, ואומרים שהוא דבר שאין לו דמות ולא צורה,
והוא מזומן ומעותד לקבל דמות וכל צורה. והשני קוראים לו צורה ואומרים
שהוא דבר שיש לו כח וגבורה להלביש את ההיולי כל דמות וכל תמונה.
וההיולי הוא חלש ודל מהיות לו כח להעמיד את עצמו ולמלאות את חסרונו
אם אין הצורה נדבקת בו, והצורה אינה יכולה להראות אל העין או לחיות אחד
מחושי הגוף מכיר אותה אם אינה מלבשת את ההיולי הסובל אותה. ותמצא
כל אחד מהם צריך אל השני ומזומן להועיל לו להמצא או להראות לבני

העולם. לולי הצורה לא היה ההיולי מתקיים ולא נמצא, ולולי ההיולי לא היתה
הצורה נראת לבני העולם. אלא שהצורה גדולה במעלה מן ההיולי מפני שאינה
צריכה אל ההיולי כי אם לגלותה ולהראותה, והיא יכולה להתקיים מעצמה
ואם אינה נגלית ולא נראית, ואין ההיולי יכול להתקיים מעצמו וגם אינה
נגלית בשום פנים כי אם בעזר הצורה. זו היא פירושו בדרך התלותן. וכל
אחד מהם בפני עצמו נחלק לשני חלקים, ושני חלקי ההיולי הן שיש ממנה
זך ונקי, ויש ממנה טינופת ושמרים. ושני חלקי הצורה שיש ממנה צורה
סתומה וחתומה, וטהורה מהדבק אל ההיולי וקדושה מהתחבר בו, והחלק השני
צורה חלולה ופתוחה וראויה להדבק אל ההיולי ולהתחבר אליו ולהתהפך בו.
וזו הצורה המתקיימת בעצמה הטהורה מדבק אל ההיולי, מציץ וזורח על הצורה
החלולה ועוזר אותה להלביש את ההיולי כל הצורות אשר הוא יכול להתכסות
בהן. והיו שני השרשים האלה שהם ההיולי והצורה גנוזים לפני המקום
ועומדים על סדריהם, עד העת אשר היה ראוי לפניו להוציאם. והמעשה והעת
אשר נאמר כאן הוא נאמר על הרחבת הלשון ועל דרך בני אדם, אבל על האמת
והעיקר אין לפני יצירת הנמצאים מן הכח אל המעשה שום עת ולא זמן. כי
הזמן היה עומד בכח בעמדת כל הנמצאות בו, [כי] אין הזמן דבר שיש לו ממש
ואינו כי אם אמידת מעמדת הנמצאות, ואם שם נמצאות אין שם אמידה
שהזמן תלוי. והם אומרים כשעלה על המחשבה הטהורה להוציאם אל המעשה,
חזק את הצורה הסתומה להתקיים ולהתלבש בזיוה שאין ההיולי נוגע בה,
והצורה הזאת אשר אינה מתדבקת אל ההיולי הוא צורת המלאכים והשרפים
והנפשות וכל הצורות המיוחסות אל העולם העליוני. והצורות אין כל בני אדם
יכולין [לראות] אותם ולא להקים צורתם בלב, מפני שאינן נדבקות אל דבר
שהעין שולטת בו ורב העולם אינם מבינם דבר שאין חושי הגוף נוגעים.
והמבינים את תוכן הצורות האלה וסדר תמונתן, הם המעמיקים בחכמה והמכירים
את כל דרכיה. ואמת שהצורה הזאת היתה היתה עומדת על תכונה והאור זהיר בתוכה
והיה אורה מפיץ על הצורה הראויה להדבק אל ההיולי והחזיקה במאמר
השם הקדוש וגבורתו להתחבר. והיתה מתחברת בראשונה אל ההיולי זך ונקי,
והיתה חבורה בו בחבור חזק וותיק שאין לו תמורה והפוך כל ימי הדבקם. ומן
הדבוק הזה נוצרו גופי הרקיעים. והיתה הצורה אחריהן מתחברת בשמרי
ההיולי וטינופן. ונוצרו מן הדבוק כל הגופות הנמצאות בעולם הממירות את
צורתן ואינם ממירות את מעמדם על חילופי מניניהן, כגון ארבע [יסודות]

שהן ארץ ומים ורוח ואש, וכל הנמצא מחבוריהם עד גדולי הארץ וצמח
האדמה. ואתה מוצא את כל גדוליהם, דבריהם המפורשים עד המקום הזה
לקוחים מדברי תורה ושאובים ממעין החכמה אם אתה מעיין בהם, ותמצא
ההיולי והצורה אשר היו לדבריהם עומדים בכח לפני בריאות העולם, הן
תהו ובהו אשר העידה התורה שהיתה הארץ. אבל כל העולם היה עומד עליהם
לפני צאתו אל המעשה במאמר הקדוש כדכתיב (בראשית א) והארץ היתה
תהו ובהו, ואם אתה מקיש פי' שם ההיולי שאמרו עליו שאין לו לא דמות ולא
צורה ואינו יכול להתקיים מעצמו אל טעם התהו, תמצאם יוצאים יחד אל ענין
אחד. כי התהו הוא דבר שאין לו שום ערך ולא חששא ולא ממש ולא תועלת,
כדכתיב (שמואל א, יג) כי אחרי התהו אשר לא יועילו ולא יצילו כי תהו המה,
כלומר אשר אין בהם כח להועיל לנפשם ולא לאחרים כי תהו המה ואין לו
קיימא לא דמות ולא צורה. וכתיב (ישעיה מה) לא תהו בראה לשבת יצרה.
להודיעך כי התהו אין לו קיימא ולא יישוב. וכל אשר אמרו בהיולי אתה יכול
לומר על תהו. ואמרו על הצורה שהוא דבר שיש לו גבורה להלביש את ההיולי
דמות וצורה. ומלת בוהו מתפרדת על הטעם הזה לשני ענינים, מפני שהיא
בנויה למשמע הלשון מן שתי אותיות או מן שתי מילים האחד בו והשני הו.
ואמר הכתוב תהו ובהו כלומר שאין לו חששא ולא קיימא ודבר אחר אשר בו
יהיה התהו מתקיים. ויהיה בהו הצורה המכסה את התהו והמקיימת אותו. ואתה
מביא ראיה מן הכתוב (ישעיה לד) ונטה עליה קו תהו ואבני בהו. והקו אין
בו תועלת במשקולת הבנין כי אם למשוך את כובד האבן המראה את תיקון
הבנין או עיותו. ומפני זה הלוה הכתוב את זה אל תוהו שנאמר (שם) קו תוהו.
והלוה האבן אל בוהו אמר אבני בוהו, מפני שהאבן מודיע יושר המשקל או
קלקולו כאשר הצורה מתקנת דמות הנוצר. ואמר קו תהו בלשון יחיד, מפני
שהצורות באות על הלובש אותו על תמונות רבות.

ואני אומר עוד כאשר אמרתי לאלתר. שמלת בוהו נחלקת לשני מילים
האחת בו והשנית הו, מפני שהצורה הנקיה הסתומה והטהורה מתקיימת
מעצמה ואינה צריכה לעזר. ויהיה טעם בוהו כאלו אמר הדבר אשר הוא
מעצמו מתקיים ובכחו מתגבר, ואם אינו מחובר אל דבר אחר. ויהיה זה
טעם תהו ובהו על כל הטעמים אשר אמרו חכמי המחקר.

העמוד הרביעי

ולפרש הטעם הזה אנו אומרים כי פעולת שמע מתפרשת בלשון הקדש
לפי הצרך לנו במקום הזה על שלש לשונות, מן שמע האזן אשר אינו בביאת
הטעם הענין, כגון לשמע אזן שמעתיך (איוב מ"ב) [וישמע אברם כי נשבה
אחיו] (בראשית י"ד), והשנית מלשון קבול עצה והמאמר, כגון וישמע יעקב
אל אביו וגו׳ וישמע אברם לקול שרי (שם), ושמעו לקולך (שמות ג׳), לא תאבה
לו ולא תשמע אליו (דברים י"ג), והשלישית מלשון בינה, שנאמר דבר נא
אל עבדיך ארמית כי שומעים אנחנו (ישעי׳ ל"ז) תשמע חלום לפתור אותו
(בראשית מ"א) כלומר תבין פתרונו. ופעלת ושמעת ושבת אשר בפסוק ושבת
עד ה׳ אלהיך ושמעת בקולו, הוא מן הלשון השלישית לאשר הוא לשון בינה,
ואינו לשון קבלה כמשמע הפעולה ברוב המקומות, כלומר תבין את קולו אשר
שמעת מתוך האש אשר אמר עליו קול דברים אתם שומעים, כלומר אתם
שומעים ומקבלים את הקול לפי פשוטו ותמונה אינכם רואים בעין לבבכם
ולא מבינים תמונת הקול וצורתו הפנימית, ואינכם מבינים זולת הקול הנשמע,
שנאמר ותמונה אינכם רואים זולתי קול (דברים ד׳). הקול היוצא מפי הגבורה
הוא לעולם הזה לאחד משני ענינים, הוא לגזור ולקים הדבר היוצא מפי
הגבורה, כגון ויאמר אלהים יהי אור, ושאר המאמרות הנבראות בהן העולם,
והוא באה להזהיר ולצוות, כגון שאמר לאדם הראשון מכל עץ הגן אכול תאכל
ומעת הדעת טוב ורע לא תאכל ממנו.

ואנו אומרים כי עשרת הדברים הנשמעים לכל ישראל מהר סיני הם
נאמרים לשני העינים האלה, היותו העינים נשמעים ומקובלים ולנהוג עליהם.
והיה משמע לא יהיה לך אלהים אחרים על פני ושאר הדברים הבאים אחריו,
אל תהי נוהג כמו המנהג הזה כמשמע המצוה והזהרה, והיו כל ישראל נוהגים
בהם מימי מתן תורה עד הישועה, [מהן] היה בהן שמקבלין ועושין כהוגן ומהן
עושין שלא כהוגן, ומשם היה בהן זכאים וחיבים. וכוונתו יתברך שמו באחרונה
לגזור אותם ולקיימם. והיה משמע לא יהיה לך אלהים אחרים על פני לא יתכן
היות הדבר הזה לעולם, ומפני זה יהיו כל ישראל מימי הישועה ולהלן מוכרחים
ומוכנים לקבל את התורה כהוגן ולא יהיה בהן יכולת ולא ינתן כח ולא
רשות לעבור עליה, כאשר אין כח בכל הנבראים לעבור הנגזרים עליהם
גזרה חתומה. ויהיו כל ישראל בימים ההם נוהגים מנהג הצדיקים הנבדלים

למרום, כאשר פרשנו רוב דרכם בתחלת דברינו. והכתוב מפרש הענין הזה ומדתו בבירור. שהוא אומר אחר הכתובים אשר הזכרנו למעלה, ומל ה' אלהיך את לבבך ואת לבב זרעך לאהבה את ה' אלהיך בכל לבבך ובכל נפשך למען חייך (דברים ל'), מפני שהקב"ה מסיר את הקושי ואת הערלה אשר היה מונע אתכם להבין את הקול על כל דרך שהוא מתפרש אליהן. ואומר למען חייך, כלומר למען חיי העולם הבא אשר כלו חיים. ולפני הכתוב הזה הוא אומר לאהבה את ה' אלהיכם ולעבדו בכל לבבכם ובכל נפשכם, ובחתימת הפרשה הוא אומר למען ירבו ימיכם וימי בניכם על האדמה, כשאתם אוהבים את ה' אלהיכם בכל לבבכם ובכל נפשכם מפני מצותו ונוהגים כפי רצונו המצליח לכם העולם הזה אשר נשתנה מדרך בריתו בעבור עון האדם, הוא מצליח את דרכו ומתקנו ומשתנה כשאדם משנה את דרכיו. אבל עתה כשאתם אוהבים מתוך גזרתי וממאמרי העולם מצליח כדרכו אשר בראתיו עליה, לא מפני הצלחת מעשה בני אדם, ולא נשאר בעבורכם שכר שתהיו מקבלים אותו על עבודתכם, כי אם חיי העולם הבא, ומשם אמר הכתוב האחרון למען חייך לא דבר אחר. ותלה הזכות בכתוב הראשון בעניני העולם הזה, שנאמר ונתתי מטר ארצכם בעתו (שם י"א), ולבסוף למען ירבו ימיכם. ואתה מוצא בראש הענין הזה בנבואת ירמיהו שהוא אומר, הנה ימים באים נאם ה' וכרתי את בית ישראל ואת בית יהודה ברית חדשה (ירמי' ל"א), הימים האלה הם ימי הגאולה אשר אנו מקוים ביאתה בקרוב ברחמי שמים אשר יהיו כל גלות ישראל ויהודה נגאלים, ואומר (שם) לא כברית אשר כרתי את אבותם ביום החזיקי בידם להוציאם מארץ מצרים אשר המה הפרו את בריתי ואנכי בעלתי בם נאם ה'. כלומר אשר המה הפרו את בריתי מפני שנתתי רשות יראת שמים ומעשים טובים בידם, ואני בעלתי בהם, שלא היו מקיימים את מצותי כהוגן. ואומר אחר כן, כי זאת הברית אשר אכרת את בני ישראל אחר הימים ההם, כלומר אחרי הגלות ההוא, ונתתי את תורתי בקרבם ועל לוח לבם אכתבנה, תחת אשר כתבתי לאבותם על לוחות האבן אני כותב אותה על לוח לבם, ותהיה נרשמת בתוך לבם ולא תשכח מפיהם. ואחריו הוא אומר והייתי להם לאלהים והם יהיו לי לעם ולא ילמדו עוד איש את רעהו ואיש את אחיו לאמור דעו את ה' כי כלם ידעו אותי למקטנם ועד גדולם, נאם ה' כי אסלח לעונם ולחטאתם לא אזכר עוד.

ואתה מוצא כלל כל הנחמה הזאת הטובה שהקב"ה מאבד יצר הרע

ומכריתו מן העולם. ויהיו כל המאמינים בשם מאמינים בו מימי קטנותם
ונערותם, עד ימי זקנותם, ויהיה הקב"ה סולח לכל עונות הקדמונים מאדם
הראשון ולהלן כשהוא יתברך שמו מתקן את לב אדם אשר הי' רע מנעוריו.
והוא מפרש הענין הזה על דרך אחרת ע"י יחזקאל, ואומר ונתתי לכם לב
חדש ורוח חדשה אתן בקרבכם, [והסירותי את לב האבן מבשרכם ונתתי לכם
לב בשר ואת רוחי אתן בקרבכם] ועשיתי את אשר בחוקי תלכו ומשפטי תשמרו
ועשיתם (יחזקאל ל"ו), בכתוב הראשון הוא נותן להם לב חדש ורוח חדשה,
שני הדברים, לב ורוח, שהיו בהם על מנהג אחר ועל צורה אחרת. והוא מפרש
את הלב הישן אשר הוא מסיר מבשרם וקורא אותו אבן, שנאמר והסירותי
את לב האבן מבשרכם.

ואנו רואים לחקור איך לבות בני אדם בעולם הזה דומות לאבן, ואומר,
כל אברי הגוף בעת שאדם יכול להשתמש באבר ההוא או נזקק להשתמש בו,
אינו צריך ללמדו ולא להנהיגו [כי] בדרך אשר נברא האבר ההוא בעצמו נוהג
כדרכו בלא למוד, כגון שאתה אומר, הרגל ברא הקב"ה להלוך, והיד לאחוז
ולמשוך והאזן לשמוע והעין לראות, והלב להבין ולדעת, וכן [כל] אבר ואבר
נברא להיות מועיל לאדם בדבר ידוע ומוכן לו, וכל אבר ואבר מקיים את
מלאכתו הנתונה לו בכל זמן שאדם צריך אליו, ואין אחד מן האברים נזקק
ללמוד סדר המעשה הנתן לו ולא להרגילו עליו כי אם הלב לבדו אשר אינו
יכול לקיים [את מלאכתו אם לא יהיה אדם] מנהיגו או מרגילו, ומן ההרגל
ההוא יהי' קונה בה או רוח להבין, ואם אתה מרגילו יכול להנהיג עצמו ואת
שאר כחות הגוף אשר הם תלויים בו. והרוח הזה אשר יהיה קונה יהיה טוב
או רע והוא מנהגת הלב כפי ענינה הן טוב הן רע. והלב דומה לענין הזה
לאבן אשר אין בה כח לזוז ממקומה ולא להחליף את צורתה, והאדם מוליכה
ומחליף את צורתה כפי רצונו. וכן הלב אין בו כח למשול ברוחו ולא להמיר
את ענינו על הדרך אשר מלמדו ומנהיגו הוא נוהג והולך, ואין שאר האברים
כן, כי הכח הנתון להם ראשונה הם שולטים עליו ומושלים בו, ואין צריכים
לעזר, ומפני זה היה זה הלב דומה לאבן וראוי להקרא אבן, וכשהקב"ה מסיר
ממנו דמות האבן ומנהיגו מנהג שאר אברי הגוף השולטים על הכח הנתון
בהן הוא קורא אתו בשר בדמות שאר אברי הגוף, ככתוב ונתתי לכם לב בשר.
ולא הזכיר את צורת הרוח הישנה אשר הוא מסיר מהם ונותן להם תחתיה
רוח חדשה, כאשר הזכיר טבע הלב הישן אשר קראו אבן, מפני שהרוח אשר

הלב קונה בעולם הזה דבר שהוא נמצא כן בשעת בריאתו, כי אם דבר שהוא
בא אליו מבחוץ וקונה אותו מלמוד בני אדם והרגלו. אם תרצה אמור שהוא
דבר עומד בו בכח, והרגל בני אדם ולמודם מוציאו למעשה, והקב"ה בימי
הגאולה הוא מוציא הרוח אשר היה בלבות בני עמו בכח ומזומן אל אחת
משני ענינים ומעמידו במעשה וממציאו אל הטוב הענין לבדו. ככתוב ואת
רוחי אתן בקרבכם, כלומר רוחי הטובה והישרה, ויהיה הלב שולט על הרוח
ההוא כמנהג שאר האברים, ולא יהיה צריך להרגילו ולא לתור כאשר היה
מנהגו לפני החדוש הזה. ככתוב ועשיתי את אשר בחקי תלכו ומשפטי תשמרו
ועשיתם, תחת צורת היראה ועבודת השם, וכל מנהג הטוב נמצא בכח המעשה
אשר יהיה הקב"ה נוטע יראתו וקדושת שמו בלבם ולא יהיו מסורים בידי
אדם כאשר היו בתחלה. ויהיו כל הנמצאים בעלם הזה בעת ההיא והם עמו
ישראל לבדם וכל הנלוים אליהם, כאשר למדנו מן הכתובים אשר דרשנו
למעלה, נוהגים מנהג אחד באמונה ובידאה, ויהיו כמה מצות נוהגות על ידיהם
וכתובות על לוח לבם ונמצאות בפיהם, ובמעשה הזה יהיו כל עניני העולם
הזה נוהגים מנהג ישר. והראיה על זה גלויה היא לעינים לכל מבין בתורה,
ככתוב ואהבת לרעך כמוך. והמצוה הזאת תהיה נוהגת ומקיימת לכל יושבי
העולם בימי הגאולה. ואם כל ישבי הארץ יהיו אוהבים איש את רעהו כאהבתו
לנפשו, בידוע שהקנאה והשנאה והחמוד יהיה נאבד מן העולם, ואלו הם
הגורמים למלחמה להרג בעולם הזה. מיכן אמר הכתוב על זמנו של משיח
וכתתו חרבותם לאתים וחניתותיהם למזמרות לא ישא גוי אל גוי חרב. ומן
המצוה הזאת לבדה נזהר מחמשה לאוין שהן מחזיקת מחיצות כל מצות שבתורה
והן מן דבור לא תרצח עד סוף עשרת הדברות.

4. JOSEPH IBN ZADDIK

DEFINITION OF PHILOSOPHY AS A MAN'S KNOWLEDGE
OF HIMSELF

EVALUATION

Defining philosophy as a study of man's knowledge of himself, Joseph ibn Zaddik named his philosophical treatise *Olam Katan (Microcosm)*. Man as a "miniature cosmos," constitutes the coherent basis and frame of reference for all inquiry. Such a definition, he argued, does not limit or circumscribe the enterprise. On the contrary, philosophy thus contrived, is the science of sciences and the end thereof, because it is the path to a knowledge of the Creator and the key to the knowledge of all.

Accordingly, knowledge of divine attributes is determined from the point of view of man's perspective of God's activities. Ibn Zaddik writes in *Olam Katan (Mikrokosmos,* 2, p. 57., ed. S. Horovitz), "The manner in which men come to apply attributes to God may be described as follows: They looked at the work of God and, therefrom, inferred the fact of His existence. Then they reflected on the work which He has brought into existence and found that it was not weak, and so they described the Creator as mighty, using this word of ordinary human speech only to convey the idea that He is not weak. They found his works perfect, and they called him wise. They perceived that he was self-sufficient, without need of anything, and hence without any motives for doing wrong. Hence they called him righteous. And so on with the other attributes. All this they did in order that people may learn from him and imitate his ways. But we must not forget that all these expressions of God's attributes are figurative."[1]

Likewise, divine nearness or distance from us is conditional upon man's position. "Do not imagine," says Ibn Zaddik, "that the Almighty is either near or removed. The notion of God's abandonment or aloofness is found only in the hearts of fools." The reason for this is, according to our philosopher, that since God's aloofness or nearness requires change of position, and position is in the category of accident, it cannot apply to God. For accidents are not applicable to God.

Ibn Zaddik did not limit himself to any specific philosophic source. His treatise, the *Olam Katan* is a compendium of philosophy, science and theology, projecting a summary of physics, psychology, metaphysics and ethics in order to give us an idea of the position of man in the world that he may realize his destiny for which he was created. As a microcosm, man has in him represented all the elements of the universe. His body is similar to the corporeal world. His rational soul resembles the spiritual world seeking "perfection and permanent good" by means of knowledge of God and the performance of His Will.

After classifying the process of knowledge first, from the point of view of sense and intellect[2] and secondly, from the perspective as necessary knowledge (such as perceptual data, self-evident truths or axioms, and traditional truths) and demonstrated, mediate knowledge built upon necessary knowledge and derived from it by means of logical inference, Ibn Zaddik proceeds to discuss the principles of the corporeal and spiritual world. He concludes the first division of the treatise by comparing the outer world (macrocosm) and man (microcosm). Knowledge of God and the permanent good is attained concomitantly with the true knowledge of himself.

According to Maimonides, in a letter to Samuel ibn Tibbon, Ibn Zaddik modelled his work on the Encyclopedia of the Brethren of Purity[3] which was essentially neo-platonic —combining Aristotelian physics with Platonic metaphysics, psychology and ethics. Detailed accounts of the sources of Ibn Zaddik are given in two works: S. Horovitz, *Der Mikrokosmos des Josef ibn Saddik*, Breslau, 1903, and Max Doctor, *Die Philosophie des Josef ibn Zaddik*, Munster, 1895.

A philosophical study of his work, however, which focuses on the central thesis of the author indicates that he was an authentic personalist who incorporated into his scheme categories that contributed to his notion of philosophy as man's knowledge of himself. He was not an eclectic compiling indiscriminately from a variety of sources in order to prove that Jews could also reason correctly. His attempt to tone down the extremes of neo-platonic tendencies and create a construct in which Aristotelianism and Platonism may meet is evidence of his genuinely independent creative scheme, designed to project a distinct discipline. In this pursuit, he left out all that he regarded as unessential or objectionable to his central thesis. While others, like the Mutakalimum, may strive to gain the permanent good and perfection (which in Plato are of the transcendent domain) by means of natural experience, requiring a preliminary knowledge of mathematics, geometry, music and astronomy, Ibn Zaddik shifted the focus on knowledge that bears directly on human experience. Self-knowledge is the highest science that leads to a knowledge of God and His Will. When man actualizes himself he is near to God. For God's nearness or aloofness is conditioned by man's self-realization. A cognitive kinship with God is the path to perfection and permanent good.

We know very little of the early life of Joseph Ibn Zaddik. Reliable sources indicate, however, that he was a Talmudist of high repute and in 1138 was appointed *Dayyan* (Judge) of the Jewish Community at Cordova, Spain,[4] Until his death in 1139 he occupied the position jointly with Maimon, the father of Maimonides.

Ibn Zaddik was also a gifted poet and some of his liturgical poems are incorporated in the Sephardic and African Mahzorim.[5] He is known chiefly for his philosophical treatise *Olam Katan* written originally in Arabic and, according to S. Horovitz, translated into Hebrew by an unknown author.[6] The original Arabic treatise was lost and we are indebted to the unknown Hebrew translator for our knowledge of this significant work.

JOSEPH Ibn ZADDIK'S INTRODUCTION TO
OLAM KATAN

Praised be the Lord, Who has endowed us with speech in order to praise Him and has set fixed times for us to extol His Unity. He is the absolute unity Who alone deserves to be worshipped. He created man and endowed him with wisdom above all other creatures as we read in scriptures, "Who teacheth us more than the beasts of the earth, and maketh us wiser than the fowls of heaven" (Job 35:11).

After this preliminary praise to the Almighty, would that He be gracious to thee, my dear pupil, for inquiring of me about the real intention of the philosophers when they use the terms permanent good and perfection. On the one hand, they tell us that perfection and permanent good are not of this world and yet they maintain that every man of intelligence should seek them. The subject matter is, indeed, very difficult and wearisome, made so by the small number of persons pursuing it and engaging in its study. This is especially true of our generation which is far inferior to the former generations, in that many people are completely devoid of the merits of knowledge and the method of investigation.

Two fundamental requisites are necessary for the knowledge of our subject. They include awareness of God and performance of His Will. This is, in truth, corroborated by King David's admonition "And thou, Solomon my son, know thou the God of thy father and serve Him with an entire heart and with a willing soul" (Chronicles I 28:9). He, moreover, indicated that by our neglect to seek Him and to know Him, He will remove Himself and His Will from us as we read: "If thou seek Him, He will let Himself be found by thee; but if thou forsake Him, He will cast thee off forever" (*ibid.*).

Do not imagine, however, that the Almighty is either near or removed, attached or aloof from any object; nor is He subject to change, perception, relation or any of the other generic or compound accidents. The notion of God's abandonment or aloofness is found only in the hearts of fools and in slumbering, indolent minds, intoxicated with lust which is worse than being inebriated from wine. This is what the philosophers refer to when they speak of the hearts of men in pursuit of lust whose minds are far removed from the Creator.

My love for wisdom and for those who pursue it has given me, therefore, no way out but to fulfill your request and do your bidding, confident that the Almighty, blessed be His name, will reward me.

I discovered that the path to this profound knowledge is to understand the works of the philosophers and theologians. But I learned that there is no way to comprehend their works without an acquaintance with the four preliminary sciences. The first is the science of arithmetic; the second, the science of geometry; the third, the science of music; and the fourth, astronomy, that is, the course of the spheres. After all these courses one should study the science of logic including the exercise of premises and syllogisms. Such a course of study takes a long time and is likely to weary the student, especially the beginner who is anxious to derive prompt benefit from his studies and digest only the salient points.

I have made it, therefore, my purpose to explain how a man can know himself, for from a knowledge of self he will come to a knowledge of all. For one who knows his self may know things outside himself but to be ignorant of one's self is surely to be ignorant of everything else. Man is, therefore, called a microcosm—a world in miniature — for he has in him represented all the elements of the universe. His body represents the corporeal world; his rational soul is like the spiritual world. This is what the philosophers meant when they attempted to limit the discipline of philosophy by defining *philosophy as a man's knowledge of himself.* For knowledge of self leads to an understanding of all, namely, the corporeal and spiritual world. This is then the science of philosophy, which is the science of sciences, and the end thereof because it is the sure path to a knowledge of the Creator and Cause of all. May He be blessed and exalted!

My purpose in this work was to be concise and to present

the subject matter in a simple manner. I refrained from indulging in difficult and lengthy discussions lest they induce weariness and rejection of the subject matter. It was necessary to introduce the subject with appropriate preliminary remarks that serve as a key and exposition to the rest. To be sure, I do not pretend to cover the entire subject or to probe its essence and all its characteristics, for this is not within my competence or inclination.

I pray that the Almighty may help me and guard me from sin for only he is safe whom the Creator safeguards, as it is written, "Yet they that wait upon the Lord shall acquire new strength, they shall mount up with wings as eagles" (Is. 40:31).

I called this work "Microcosm" for it touches upon the crucial question we have raised and the main purpose toward which we directed our attention. I have divided the treatise into four divisions. The first part treats of premises and introductory hypotheses necessary for our exposition. Also included is a classification of the various species in the corporeal world which are changeable and have no permanence.

The second division deals with man's knowledge of himself as a microcosm and the reasons that philosophers refer to him as such. The third is devoted to doctrines and principles in reference to God. The fourth part constitutes our exposition on ethics as well as the nature of transgressions and reward and punishment thereof.

Now that I have enumerated the number of divisions in the book, following, as I am wont to do, in the footsteps of the philosophers and emulating their wise methods, we shall revert to the task set for ourselves and proceed to expound upon the purpose toward which we strive, with confidence and trust in our God as we find "those who know Thy name put their trust in Thee, for Thou hast not forsaken those who seek Thee, O Lord" (Psalm 9:11).[7]

ספר העולם הקטן

לר׳ יוסף אבן צדיק

תהלה לאל אשר נתן ללשונות מבטא להללו וקבען להודות יחודו, הוא
האחד הפשוט אשר ראוי לעבדו לבדו, אשר ברא את האדם והשכילו יותר משאר
בעלי חיים כאשר בא בכתוב (איוב ל״ה, י״א) מלפנו מבהמות ארץ ומעוף
השמים יחכמנו יתברך ויתעלה למעלה מכל ברכה, אשר שהקדמנו תהלת האל
יתברך, יחנך האל התלמיד הותיק הנעים לפי ששאלת ממני מה היא כוונת
החכמים באמרם הטוב המתמיד והמעלה השלמה ואמרו שהמעלה ההיא והטוב
ההוא אינם מצואים בעולם הזה ואמרו שדבר זה ראוי לדרוש אחריו לכל בעל
שכל וראיתי הדרך הזה שיש בה יגיעה גדולה והוא דבר קשה להשיגו למיעוט
התרים אחריו והמבקשים אותו כ״ש בדורנו זה שהוא דור ריק ופחות מכל
הדורות שעברו ואף כי ידיעת ענין זה שהוא אפס מהם. והדרך להשיג בקשה
זו יצטרך שני עקרים גדולים האחד מהם ידיעת הבורא יתברך והשני עשות
רצונו כאשר יתחייב מדרך האמת וכמאמר דוד ע״ה (ד״ה א׳ כ״ח, ט׳) ועתה
שלמה בני דע את אלהי אביך ועבדהו ועוד כתוב בתורת משה (דברים ד׳ כ״ט)
ובקשתם משם את ה׳ אלהיך ומצאת כי תדרשנו וגו׳ ואמר כי בעזבנו בקשתו
ובקשת ידיעתו יתרחק ממנו וירחיק ממנו רצונו שנאמר (דה״י שם) אם תדרשנו
ימצא לך ואם תעזבנו יזניחך לעד. לא תעלה בדעתך שהוא רחוק מדבר וקרוב
לדבר ולא ידבק ולא יתפרד ולא ישיגהו שנוי ולא דמות ולא ערך ולא שום
עניני המקרים הכלליים והפרטיים הדבקים במקרים לבד כי העזיבה הזאת
והרחוק הזה הוא דבק ללבבות הפתאים והנפשות הנרדמות תרדמת העצלות
השכורות מתאות העולם הזה ששכרותו רע ומאוס משכרות היין ובעניין הזה
אמרו הפילוסופים הלבבות הרודפים אחר התאוות שכלם רחוק מהבורא ית׳
ולא היה לי דרך להנצל מתת בקשתך ומעשות שאלתך לאהבתי בחכמה ובכל
המבקשים אותה ואבטח להשיג שכר מהבורא ית׳ שמו. וראיתי שהדרך לזאת
הידיעה הגדולה הנוראה הוא לעמוד על ספרי הפילוסופים הטהורים והחכמים
האלהיים רצון צורם עליהם. וראיתי שאין דרך למשתוקק לעמוד על ספרים

אלו כ"א להרגיל עצמו בחכמות ארבע שאחת מהם היא הארתמאתקי והיא
חכמת החשבון והשנית אל הנדסה והיא חכמת התשבורת והשלישית מוסיקי
והיא חכמת חיבור הניגון והרביעית היא התכונה ואחר כל זה ללמוד חכמת
המבטא וההקשיות השכליות. וראיתי כל זה שיצטרך בלמודו לזמן מרובה ויקוץ
התלמיד כל שכן המתחיל שרצונו למהר תועלתו ולקחת מהחכמה המובחר
ממנה. ושמתי כוונתי לבאר ידיעת האדם אמתת עצמו לפי שמידיעתו לעצמו
ידע הכל ומי שידע עצמו אפשר שידע את זולתו ומי שלא ידע עצמו כ"ש
שלא ידע זולתו. ועל כן נקרא האדם עולם קטן לפי שיש בו דמות לכל מה
שבעולם. גופו במעלת העולם הגשמי ונפשו החכמה במעלת העולם הרוחני.
ובענין זה אמרו הפילוסופים בשומם חק ורשם לפילוסופיא כי הפילוסופיא
היא ידיעת האדם נפשו כי מידיעתו נפשו ידע הכל ר"ל עולם הנשמות ו[ה]עולם
הרוחאני וזאת היא חכמת הפילוסופיא שהיא חכמת החכמות ותכליתן לפי
שהיא מדרגה ושביל לידיעת בורא הכל ומתחילו ית' ויתעלה. ושמתי כוונתי
בכל זה אל דרך הקיצור והקרוב מיראתי הדרכים העמוקים הארוכים שזה יביא
האדם לקוץ בחכמה ולמאוס אותה. והקדמתי קודם מה שראוי להקדים להיות
כמפתח והצעה לזולתו ובכל זה איני מתפאר להשיג כל הענין ולא לרדת
לאמתתו לכל הראוי בו כי אין זה מיכלתי ואינו מטבעי ואני אבקש מאשר לו
הגבורה ומאתו העזרה שיעזרני ויאמצני וישמרני מחטוא בלשוני, ומהיותי
אשם וידעתי כי אשר ישמרנו הבורא הוא השמור כאשר בא בכתוב (ישעי'
מ', ל"א) וקוי ד' יחליפו כח יעלו אבר כנשרים וגו' וקראתי שם חבורי זה
ספר עולם קטן הואיל והגענו לשאלתנו אשר שאלנו וכוונתנו אשר התכוונו
אליה וחלקתי החיבור הזה לארבעה מאמרות.

המאמר הראשון בהקדמות והצעות אליהם להבא ובמיני העולם הזה
הגשמי ושהוא חולף אין לו עמידה.

המאמר השני בידיעת האדם עצמו ושהוא עולם קטן ומה הענין אשר
בשבילו קראוהו החכמים הפילוסופים עולם קטן.

המאמר השלישי בעיקרים וכללים מחכמת האלהות.

המאמר הרביעי בביאור כללים מן מעשים טובים ומעברות זהגמול
והעונש ואמתתם והואיל ומנינו מנין המאמרות של ספר כמנהג הפילוסופים
לאהבתי לצאת בעקביהם וללמוד ממיטב פעולותיהם נשוב להשלים מה שיעדנו
ונבאר הכוונה אשר אלי' התכוונו והבטחון והתקוה באל הגדול דכתיב (תהלים
ט' י"א) ויבטחו בך יודעי שמך כי לא עזבת דורשיך ה'.

5. MOSES IBN EZRA

SELF-KNOWLEDGE AS THE AUTHENTICATION OF
HUMAN EXISTENCE

EVALUATION

The foremost medieval Jewish philosopher to incorporate neo-platonic thought-forms in his intellectual mode of discourse was Solomon ibn Gabirol. Because the Jewish neo-Platonists drew their philosophical notions in the main from him, they did not have to construct their own ideological system but simply based their psychological and ethical expositions on certain elements of Gabirol's metaphysics.

Moses ibn Ezra is one of them. His philosophical treatise *Arugat ha-Bosem* (Row of Spices), while consisting mostly of sayings and quotations on the neo-Platonic notions of the unknowability of God, motion, nature and intellect, its chief aim is to underscore the position and destiny of man in the universe. He maintained that the union of the corporeal and the spiritual in man makes his position unique and central in the cosmos. As a microcosm and at the same time by virtue of his spiritual endowments, "he can strip his soul of his corporeal senses and worldly desires, and rise to the sphere of the Intelligence to find his reward."

In the personalistic tradition of Jewish philosophy, Moses ibn Ezra defined the philosophic enterprise as the pursuit of self-knowledge. To know one's own self is the key to the knowledge of the Creator, which in essence constitutes the authentication of one's existence, for a cognitive relation to God is indispensable to human existence.

The neo-Platonic notion of Thought and Being as constituting the first emanation proceeding from the One and the Good Absolute Cause was attractive to the Jewish philosopher, for it tended to hypostatize an ultimate Being in the *Nous* (Reason) which embraces both principles of existence. The attainment of knowledge would lead to everlasting life (Being) in the sphere of the Intelligence where both are part of a second emanation.

The neo-Platonic scheme of emanation, as delineated by Plotinus,[1] presented at least two difficulties to Jewish philosophers. In the first place, the process of gradual and successive emanations of existences, radiating from the superabundant light and goodness of the Creator, seems to relate only to cosmic existences. For Plotinus, the Intelligence and the three souls proceeding from it in order, are clearly not individual but cosmic beings. The Jewish neo-Platonic personalist was concerned with the relation of man's rational and psychic faculties to these cosmic beings. Isaac Israeli, the first Jewish neo-Platonist, dealt with the problem and succeeding philosophers, including Moses ibn Ezra, incorporated it into their scheme. The cosmic hypostases, Israeli argued, are contained in the rational faculties of man and temporarily individualized, returning to their source after the disintegration of the body.

The second neo-Platonic concept that baffled Jewish philosophers was the notion of the absolute transcendence and unknowability of God which tended to push Him out of the affairs of the universe and substitute for Him the first emanation, the *nous*. The implications of such a scheme were obvious. They would lead to the hypostatization of the first gradation of being which alone would be involved in the governorship of the world.

Solomon ibn Gabirol met the challenge by introducing into the emanation scheme a new notion which Moses ibn Ezra adopted and related directly to man's passive intellect. It is the concept of the divine Will, as distinguished from His Essence, that gave a new perspective to God's relation to the universe and to man's central place in it. Since it is the Will of God that impresses form upon matter and thereby creates a world, God, according to Ibn Gabirol, is involved directly in the affairs of the universe. Both matter and form came from God, matter from His essence, form from His Will. In God, Who is a perfect unity, essence and will are one. From man's vantage point, however, the will is identical with God if we think of it apart from its activity; considered as active, the will is an attribute distinct from divine essence. Knowledge of God's perfect unity thus depends on man's perspective. It is from the human frame of reference—this represents Ibn Gabirol's personalistic scheme on the epistemological level—that a determination is made whether essence and attribute are one.

Moses ibn Ezra took the notion of divine will and applied it directly to man's passive intellect. "The Active Intellect is the first of God's creations. It is a power emanating from the Will. It is a simple, pure, transparent substance, bearing in itself the forms of all existing things. The human intellect is a composition related to it from the other creations and is known as the passive intellect. The rational soul is a simple substance giving perfection to a material body. It is inferior to the intellect and the animal soul is inferior to the rational."[2]

The *Arugat ha-Bosem* represents, then, a consummate development of a neo-Platonic personalism.

Moses ibn Ezra was born in Granada, Spain about 1070 and died in 1138. He was a first-rate poet and his poetic writings include secular as well as religious poetry.[3] Of his philosophical treatise *Arugat ha-Bosem,* only several extracts of a Hebrew translation published by Dukes in "Zion" 11 Frankfurt a.M., 1842, are accessible in print.

A brief passage derived from a different manuscript was also published by Dukes in *Literaturblatt des Orients,* X which is not found in *Zion.*

What follows is my translation of the first section of *Arugat ha-Bosem* as it appeared in *Zion* II pp. 117-122.

ARUGAT ha-BOSEM

The philosopher[4] said: the Eternal Creator bears no resemblance to the objects of his creation; otherwise He would not be the Creator. The men of science noted, moreover, that there is nothing above or below, the counterpart of which is not found in miniature in man, in accordance with the disposition of his nature and his body. There is no sphere or star or planet, animal or plant or mineral, nor any species of living creatures that swarm and creep after their kind, as well as every winged fowl, the beasts of the sea and anything that crawls on its belly and many-legged animals, nor is there any power, or nature but that something similar, *mutatis mutandis,* is found in man. One may even extend the list to complete the similarities.

The ten categories which, according to the philosophers, constitute the principles of all existence are also found in man. Consider, for instance, that man is included in the category of substance, for the essence of man is to speculate and to know.[5]

He likewise possesses the category of quantity as he is a creature of composition; the category of quality, as he is either white or black; the category of relation, as he is a father or son; the category of place, as he is either here or there; the category of time, as he exists in a fixed time; the category of possession, as he acquires things and possesses a household; the category of position, as he stands or sits; the category of action, as he eats and drinks; the category of passiveness, as he is born and afflicted. All of these terms find their proper expression in the Hebrew language.

While man in reality is an organic unit, his activities which are embraced by these general principles are many. Time is prior to all terrestrial creations as their very being depends on the element of time and any object upon which anything else is contingent precedes the latter in existence. Human bodies are similar to the bodies of minerals in the sense that they require space for their natural motion. They are likewise compared to plants that grow, since they wither and decay; and they are similar to animals in a variety of ways, such as in their appetitive aspects, in their display of

anger, fear and imagination. They are similar also to angels in the
exercise of their rational faculties which come from the universal
intellect or from the Creator whence it emanated.

In addition, the elements of water and earth within us tend
to move toward the center, pushing the bodies into their proper
place, while our endowments of the elements of vapor, air and
fire tend to move away from the center. Our faculties to draw
liquid and to digest food, which is deposited into our blood stream,
we share with the plants. The veins of the stomach that attract food
to the liver[6] are similar to the roots of the tree. This process is
referred to in Scriptures as "the bars of the nether-world" (Job
17:16), which also conduct and draw their nourishment of the
element of heat, to the bowels of the nether-world.

Verily, the perfection of man's creation points to a wise Creator. It is beyond the limits of wisdom and demonstration to conceive how form is impressed upon matter, called *hyle,* which bears it.
Philosophers agree that every body is composed of *hyle* and every
composition has a rational purpose. Indeed, we might say that man
alone comes after multiplicity; the exalted Creator is before multiplicity. This fact, supported by scientists, contradicts the arguments of the heretics who claim that man was created without any
purpose, but is a product of chance or fate without necessary existence and devoid of the providential care of a wise Creator.

Socrates, the metaphysician, said in his prayers: "May the
name of the Lord be praised whose works are all as they should
be without addition or diminution." What we know of the composition of man's body and the performance of his faculties and
soul and what we behold generally with our eyes about the quality
of his nature from the arts, sciences, ethics and metaphysical
knowledge (true wisdom), theoretical and practical proofs, point to
man as a microcosm. For man is like the great universe in his composition, judgment and creation. The intellectual faculty, which is
the most distinct and simplest of all the substances of the universe,
cannot come in direct contact with the corporeal, but needs the
soul and the spirit as intermediary powers to link the light substance with the heavy and the subtle with the coarse. In man, too,
soul and spirit are midway between intellect and body, for the

spiritual, because of its subtle nature, cannot be brought together with the coarse body without an intermediary. By the same token, the core of the great universe which is the most simple, distinct element, namely prime matter that bears the ten categories, cannot unite directly with the corporeal world. Indeed, as we said, man's body forms an epitome of the great universe in its entirety.

It is written, the wise men defined philosophy in the well-known three-fold manner. The first definition is derived from its etymological connotation. The second is taken from the characteristics of its aim. The third, from the nature of its activity and knowledge. The mark of its activity is for man to know himself truly—his spiritual as well as his corporeal aspects. He would then know all other spiritual and bodily powers. For in man are combined all substances—spiritual is the reason and the soul, and corporeal is the body with its dimensions of length, breadth and depth.

One of the philosophers further maintained that to boast of knowing the realities of things without first knowing one's own soul, is like a person who feeds other people while he himself is hungry. Or he may be compared to one who clothes others while he is naked; healing others while he is ill; setting up standards for others while his own household is devoid of any values.

It is, therefore, proper and appropriate that the soul understands itself in order to understand better the Creator. Without self-knowledge it is impossible to comprehend the signs of the Artisan [God] whence the soul was hewn.

It is written in ancient books of wisdom that he who can strip his soul of his corporeal senses and worldly desires and rise to the upper sphere, will find there his reward. Aristotle said: "Frequently, I retire within my soul, stripping myself of every vestige of corporeality, until I revert to a state of being all soul without body. For, then, I become absorbed with the splendor of the glow and beauty pervading me with a profound sense of mysterious wonderment until I become aware that I am part of the world of splendor." Alas, these expressions are rationally convincing experiences.

The wise Pythagoras in his ethical instructions to a disciple said: "When you will do what I tell you and remove during your life every corporeal aspect of your being and roam in the upper sphere without ever intending to return to the physical substances, then you will know you have reached your goal." One of the wise men of metaphor therefore remarked: "To be near to God requires one to deliver his soul from this world while still being a part of it."

Moreover, one of the later philosophers[7] said: If you wish to form a picture in your mind of the celestial substances, to reflect upon them, to embrace and apprehend them, you must raise your intellect to the ultimate intelligible. After you will purify your intellect from all sordid sensibility, emancipate it from the captivity of nature and approach with the force of your intelligence to the ultimate of intelligible substance that it is possible for you to comprehend, until you are entirely stripped of sensible substance and lose all feeling and knowledge thereof, then you will find the whole corporeal world stored away in your soul and embraced in your thoughts so that you can include it in one corner of your soul. When you have done this, you will behold the insignificance and deficiency of the sensible in comparison with the greatness of the intelligible. Then you will apprehend with your rational "eyes" the spiritual substances from on high and they will appear as if they are before your eyes, embracing you and superior to you, and you will see your soul as one of those spiritual substances without any difference between them and sometimes you will think you are all of them and that there is no difference between you and them on account of the identification of your being with their being. You will, then, apprehend the intellectual substances and delight in their pleasure.[8]

Moreover, you will discover that the corporeal substances in relation to this splendor are reduced to complete nothingness and diminution until you behold the corporeal world floating in the spiritual substance as a boat in the sea or a bird in the air.

The philosopher further stated that inasmuch as man's rational faculty is superior to every other part of his being, it behooves man to seek its wisdom that it may, together with its soul, act and embrace the lower substances. That is why Plato supplemented his definition of philosophy with the notion that the aim of philosophy is for man to become like God as far as possible.[9]

ליקוטים מספר ערוגת הבושם

לר' משה בן עזרא

זה מאמר העתקתי מספר ערוגת הבושם שהוא אל החכם הגדול
ר' משה בן עזרא ז"ל

אמר הפילוסוף כי הבורא הקדמון אינו דומה לדבר מנבראים ואם הוא
דומה אינו בורא. ואנשי המדע זכרו כי כל מה שיש למעלה ולמטה נמצא באדם
קצת ממנו דמיון כפי חיוב טבעו וגופו ואמרו כי אין גלגול ולא כוכב ולא מזל
ולא חי ולא צמח ולא מוצא ולא מין במין בעלי חיים השורץ והרומש עד בעל
כנפים וחיות המים וכל הולך על גחון על כל מרבה רגלים וכל כח וטבע
שיש בו שלא תמצא כמוהו בבני אדם על פי חלוף יצירתם ושנוי תמונתם
ויאריך להביא דמיונים ומשלים על זה. גם י' הכחות אשר הם עיקר המציאות
אצל הפילוסופים מצואים באדם. וזה פירושם כי האדם נכלל בשער העיון כי
הוא עין האדם המעיין והיודע ובשער הספירה כי הוא נברא מחלקים מקובצים
ובשער התואר כי הוא לבן או שחור ובשער הצטרפות כי הוא אב או בן ובשער
המקום כי הוא בכאן או במקום אחר ובשער העת כי הוא נמצא בזמן קצוב
ובשער היש כי יש לו כל וקנין ובני בית ובשער המצב כי הוא עומד או יושב
ובשער הפעול כי הוא אוכל ושותה ובשער הפעול כי הוא ילוד או מוכה
וכלם מצואים בלשון קדש. והאדם אחד אך הענינים אשר הביאוהו באלה
הכללים הם רבים. וכל ברואי הארץ נמצא הזמן קודם להם כי הוייתם הוא
מהויית הזמן וכל דבר אשר הוייתו מדבר האחר קודם לו במציאות וגוייתהן
דומות לגויות המתכות מפני שהם צריכות למקום בתנועות הטבעיות. ודומות
לצמח בגדולו באשר ימולל ויבש, ודומות אמנם לבהמות במדות רבות נפשיות
כמו התאוה והכעס והפחד ולחשוב מה שאין אמת ודומה למלאכים בפעולות
השכליות ומה שיש להם מן השכל והוא מסוד השכל הכללי או מן הבורא אשר
חנכו. ואשר בנו מן האיברים הטמים והעפריים יתנועעו לעומת האמצע וידחקו
הגופות במקומותם ואשר ישכנו מן הקטורים ורוחות והאש יתנועעו מן האמצע
ואשר ישכנו מכח שואבת המשקה ומושכת המאכל והופכות אותו לדם אלו

משתתפים בו עם הצומח כי דמיון גידי האצטומכא מושכים המזון אל הכבד
הם בה שורש האילן והם הנקראים בדי שאול (איוב י"ז, ט"ז) כי הם מושכות
ושואבות לבטן שאול מה שהם בו נזונין שיש בהן מן החום היסודי.

וכתב וגם אמנם כי כל יצור מתוקן יורה על יוצר חכם ואע"פ שנעלם
מן העין וגבול החכמה להרכיב הצורה על הכח הנושאת הנקראת היולי. ודעת
הפילוסופים הסכים כי כל גוף מורכב מהיולי וכל מורכב יש לו תכלית בהתחלת
השכל. ובאמת נאמר כי האדם לבדו הוא אחרי הרבוי הבורא רם ונשא הוא
קודם הרבוי וזה הדבר דומה לו ממופתי החכמים סותר מי שאומר שזה
הגוף נברא בלי כוונה אלא כפי מה שנזדמן או במזל אשר אין עמו לא הכרח
ולא השגחה מאת הבורא חכם אשר בראו האל למעלה מדברי הכופרים.

וכתב עוד וסוקראט האלוהי אמר בתשבחותיו ישתבח שמך האל אשר כל
מפעליו כפי הראוי להיות בלי תוספת ומגרעת. ובעבור מה שזכר מהרכבת הגוף
האדם ושמושי כחותיו ונפשו ומה שאנו רואים בכלל בעין הגוף ובתכונת יצירתו
מן המלאכות והחכמות והמדות והדעות מתושיות והאותיות הנפשיות והגשמיות
על כן נקרא האדם עולם קטן כאשר נקרא האדם העולם הגדול בעבור כי כקטן
כגדול בהרכבתו וגזרתו ובריתו ועצם השכל הנכבד והפשוט מכל עצמי כחות
העולם אינו דבק בגוף אך הנפש והרוח נכנסו באמצעות השכל עד אשר נקשר
הקל בכבד והדק בגס לבעבור עמוד הנפש המדברת בגוף ולהשאר בו בהכנת
הרוחות בינה ובין הגוף, כי אי אפשר לנפש שתעמוד בגוף לרוב דקותה וגסותו
מבלי מחבר אמצעי. ועל זה הדרך תמצא העולם הגדול ר"ל כי אין העצם
הפנימי הפשוט הנכבד מתאחד בגוף העולם וזה העצם הוא הכח הנושא לעשר
הכחות אשר זכרנו למעלה כי גוף האדם הוא דומה לגוף העולם הכללי אשר
אמרנו.

וכתב, והחכמים גבלו הפילוסופיא ב' גבולים ידועים, הא' נגזר משמה,
והב' נלקח מסגולת כחותיה, והג' מאותות פעולותיה וחכמותיה, ואותות פעולותיה
הוא שידע האדם נפשו כפי הראוי וידע כחותיו הרוחניים והגשמיים נמצא
כולל דעת שער הכחות הפנימיות והגשמיות כי הוא כלל בנפש כל החמרים
וכל הרוחניות והגשמיות. והעצם נחלק לשנים, ממנו רוחני ממנו גשם. והרוחני
כמו השכל והנפש והגשמי כגון הגוף הארוך הרחב העמק.

עוד אמר אחד מן הפילוסופים לא טוב לנו להתפאר בידיעת אמתיות
הנבראים ואנחנו לא נדע נפשנו כי כל המתפאר בזה והוא לא ידע נפשו

דומה למאכיל בני אדם והוא רעב או מכסה זולתו והוא ערום או מרפא בלעדו
והוא חולה או מורה דרך לבני איש והוא לא ידע דרך ביתו, ועל כן יאות ויכוון
כשהנפש תסכל עצמה להיותה יותר סכלה בבוראה ולא יתכן לה להבין אותות
האומן אשר הצבה עד אשר תכיר עצמה. ונמצא כתוב בחכמה הקדמונית כי כל
מי שיוכל לחלוץ גופו מעל נפשו חושיו ורגשיו מרדוף אחרי העולם ויעלה
בנפשו אל הגלגל ימצא שם גמולו. אמר אריסטו לפעמים אני מתבודד עם נפשי
ואחלוץ גופי מעלי ואשוב כאלו אני נפש בלא גו ואז אמצא מזיו הכבוד וההוד
והיופי הנאצל עלי מה שאעמיד עליו תמה ונפלא ואדע כי אני מחלקי העולם
הנכבד. ואלה הדברים הם רמזים שכליים. ופיטאגארס החכם אמר בחגורתו
המשובצת בעשותך מה שאמרתי לך אתה הוגלים ותפרד גופך בחייך לשוט
בעולם העליון מבלי שתתחזר אל כחות הגופניות דע כי השגת חפצך. ואמר
אהד מחכמי המליצה כי הקרוב מכם לבורא כל מי שיוציא נפשו מן העולם
אעפ"י שהוא שוכן בו. ואמר זולתו מן הפילוסופים האחרונים כרצותך לצייר
לעיני שכלך הכחות הפשוטות העליונות ולשוט נפשך בהם ולהיותך כולל
אותם וחופף עליהם הגבה למעלה שכלך לקצה חוג המושכלות אחר אשר
תטהר שכלך מחלאת המורגשות וגאל אותו ממאסר הטבעי ותגיע בכח שכלך
לתכלית מה שתוכל להשיג מאמתת הכחות המושכלות עד אשר כאלו נפשך
נפשטת מן החומר וכאלו אינך מרגיש בו ולא יודע אותו. ואז תמצא כל העולם
הגשמי שקוע בנפשך ונכלל במחשבותיך עד אשר תוכל לכלול אותו בזויות
מזויות נפשך. ובעשותך כן תשקיף על בוז ערך העולם המורגש וחסרונו
לנגד גדולת שפעת העולם המושכל ואת תצייר לעין שכלך הכחות הרוחניות
אשר למעלה עד אשר תראה מונחות לפניך נצבות לנגד עיניך מחופפות
עליך עומדות לנכחך ותראה נפשך כאלו היא אחד מהם מבלי הפרש ביניהם
ותחשוב כי אתה מכללם ואין הפרש בינך ובינם מרוב התאחדות עצמך
בעצמם ואז תשגיח בכחות המושכלות ותתענג בתענוגיהם. ותמצא הגופות
המורגשות כשתעריכם אל הכבוד ההוא נמצאים בתכלית החסרון והגריעות
עד אשר תראה עולם הגשמי ישוט בתוך רחב העולם הרוחני כאלו הוא
ספינה בתוך הים או עוף באויר השמים. אמר הפילוסוף אחרי אשר החלק העליון
מן האדם נכבד מכל חלקיו נדע כי ראוי לו לבקש היא החכמה והצריך
לו מן החכמה שתהא זה עם נפשו מחופפת על הכחות וכלם נכללים בתורה
מצואים תחתיה וע"כ הוסיף אפלטון בגבול הפילוסופיא ואמר כי גבול
הפילוסופיא הוא להדמות לעליון כפי יכולת האדם.

6. ABRAHAM IBN EZRA

MAN AS THE FRAME OF REFERENCE FOR ALL INQUIRY

EVALUATION

The philosophical notions of Abraham Ibn Ezra do not appear in a coherent, systematic work of philosophy. They are scattered through his writings, in his commentaries on *Tanakh*, especially in the Book of Ecclesiastes and in some of his small treatises, such as *Yesod Mora*.[1]

Abraham Ibn Ezra was born in Toledo, Spain, in 1092. His education was many-faceted. Besides philology and ex-egesis, he studied mathematics, astronomy, astrology, and re-ligious philosophy as developed by Moslems and Jews in his native land. He was also a poet of no mean order. As a philoso-pher he incorporated neo-platonic notions, following closely in the footsteps of Solomon Ibn Gabirol whom he praises as a great thinker. He was also influenced by some doctrines of Kalam, especially when he adopted the atomistic theory of Democritus as developed by Mutakallimum.[2] Of special interest is the allegorical interpretation he adopted from Philo con-cerning the Garden of Eden, the Tree of Knowledge and the river issuing from the Garden, although as a philologist he generally condemned the symbolical method of interpreting the Bible.[3]

Motivated by a crusading zeal, like his contemporary, Abraham Bar Hiyya, he left his native land and visited the

Jewish communities of Rome, London, Egypt, and Morocco.[4]
Everywhere his intention was to bring to the Jews of northern
Europe, with their emphasis on Talmudic scholarship and their
apparent disdain for philosophical speculation, a rationalistic,
scientific spirit as developed in his native Spanish Jewish community. By incorporating philosophical ideas in his commentary to the various books of the Bible, Ibn Ezra succeeded
in projecting the philosophic mode of discourse as indigenous to
Jewish tradition. To be sure, some of his ideas are only
alluded to in a cryptic manner and frequently expressed with
enigmatic brevity but their authentic biblical source could not
be denied. By the same token, a selective reading of his
biblical commentary reveals the distinctive character of personalism inherent in his ideological construct.

Ibn Ezra's personalism becomes apparent very early in his
commentary on the Bible. With respect to the very first reference to man in Genesis (1:26) "let us make man in our image,"
Ibn Ezra comments: "Now I shall explain something you should
know, namely, that the entire act of creation was for the purpose
of man in accordance with the commandment of God. At first
vegetation was brought forth by the elements of earth and water,
as were all living animals. Subsequently, God said to the
angels (intelligences) 'Let *us* make man'—indicating let *us*
engage in his creation and not the elements of water and earth
. . . Accordingly, since man's rational soul never dies it is
comparable in its eternity to God. Moreover, the soul of man
— which is incorporeal and permeates his physical existence —
together with the body of man are a microcosm of the universe
. . . And, therefore, the prophet states that 'he saw the Glory
of God as the appearance of a man'."[5]

Likewise, in his commentary on one of the later Scriptural

books (Daniel 10:21) he states: "And man alone is the foundation of the sublunar world and it is because of him that the world was created, his soul being linked to the Upper Soul (Intelligences).[6]

In these passages Ibn Ezra projects human personality as a point of departure for all inquiry by positing man as a microcosm. The essence of man is the *neshamah*. Once the soul perceived its own true nature it will apprehend how to actualize its potential by the power of intellection and come near to God. Accordingly, in his introduction to *Yesod Mora*, he writes: "Let me state at the outset that the preeminence of man over the beast is due to his rational soul, derived from on-high, which is destined to return to God who gave it."[7]

The accent on the primacy of man is further stressed in his introduction to the Ten Commandments, wherein he states that our observance of the precepts of the Torah are not for the sake of God but for our self perfection that all may be well with us all the days of our lives.[8] In the *Yesod Mora*, Ibn Ezra compares the negative commandments to the instructions of a doctor to a patient to refrain from eating certain foods and the positive commandments to a doctor's prescription of a certain diet. Just as the doctor does not benefit from such instructions but rather seeks the well-being of his patient, so, too, God does not benefit from our observing his commandments but rather desires our well-being through their observance.[9]

The importance of the intellect in the ultimate "cleaving to God" is spelled out by Ibn Ezra in his commentaries on the later prophets, Hagoiographa and his treatise on the *mitzvot*, *Yesod Mora*.

In his commentaries to some selected Scriptural passages, he writes: 'and you shall cleave to Him' — with your thoughts, so that not a minute passes without reflecting to the best of your ability upon God's marvelous works" (Hosea 3:5).[10]

"'And let us know that we may eagerly strive to know the Lord' because this is the secret behind all intellectual disciplines (i.e., knowledge of the Lord) and for this (i.e., learning about God) alone was man created. However, it is impossible to apprehend God until one has learned many preliminary sciences, which serve as a ladder to the highest level of knowledge. The expression keshakhar ("like the morning dawn") denotes that initially, the wise man will know God, blessed be He, only through his deeds, which is similar to the initial appearance of the morning dawn, but with the passage of time, the brightness of the light increases until one sees the truth clearly" (Hosea 6:3). Accordingly, knowledge of God is a gradual process. We first experience God-in-Relation and in the ultimate situation God-in-Essence.[11]

"In my opinion, the expression piryo (its fruit) refers to the rational soul which will be filled with God's Torah, so that it may recognize its Creator and His works, which last forever. It will cleave to a higher world when it has separated from the body, just as the ripened fruit separates from a tree. Now, the soul of the righteous man is like unto grain, which endures, and the wicked man is like straw before the wind" (Psalm 1:3).[12]

"It seems to me that since man is the most glorious of all creatures on earth that the Psalmist speaks thus, for as soon as a child begins to speak—and this is the explanation of the phrase "from the mouths of babes" — his intellectual faculties begin to acquire the faculty of a rational soul, until they are capable of apprehending, through reason, the power of their Creator, as the soul develops day after day . . . 'Glory and grandeur will adorn him (man)'—because of the power of the living soul which God breathed into man; it is supreme, incorporeal, and consequently, immortal." (Psalm 8:3, 6).[13]

" 'I have always set the Lord before me' — for the soul cleaves unto its Creator before it separates from the body . . . 'Thou wilt let me know the path of life' — for, when the body perishes, Thou wilt make me aware of the (correct) path of life. And the term 'path' implies the way through which I may rise to Heaven to dwell with the angels on high. And the meaning of 'fullness of joy through Thy presence,' is the joy of abiding in the radiance of the Divine Presence. And the meaning of 'Thou wilt let me know' is that Thou will strengthen the soul to withstand the mundane affairs of this world, so that it may directly perceive the truth . . . 'pleasures are at thy right hand forever' — indeed, the reward of the righteous man is explained in this Psalm . . . for once one cleaves to the Supreme Power, his soul, by virtue of this attachment will rejoice. 'As for me, in righteousness shall I behold thy face' — I have no desire other than to behold Thy presence, for the righteousness which I have stored up is the reason for my joy such as beholding Thy Presence . . . Such a vision is not experienced in a dream but occurs when one is awake. It is not a visual image but an intellectual perception, which provides a true vision of God. These are matters which can only be understood by one who has studied the wisdom of the soul" (Psalm 16:8, 11; 17:15).[14]

It is, indeed, significant that Ibn Ezra's emphasis on the power of intellection for the soul to attain its destiny applies also to the *mitzvah*. The *mitzvah*, in a personalistic perspective, habituates one to a pattern of behavior wherein he "cleaves to God" not only on a practical but also on an intellectual level. The search for *taame ha-mitzvot* (the reasons for the mitzvot) is the practice and intellection over them by which the *neshamah* rises to the Divine Presence. To fathom the divine wisdom and establish patterns of thought and behavior is conducive to coming near to God. They provide the best specific means for actualizing man's potential.

Accordingly, in his introduction to Ten Commandments and *Yesod Mora,* Ibn Ezra classifies the *mitzvot* into three categories: *mitzvot halev*—precepts involving the mind, such as love of God; *mitzvot hapeh,* precepts of the mouth, such as recital of the *Shma;* and *mitzvot hamaaseh,* precepts requiring action. However, the most important *mitzvot* are those of the mind. In *Yesod Mora,* (chapter 7) he states: "Thus, all of the *mitzvot* are of three types. First, belief of the heart, second, utterances of the mouth and third, deeds . . . The main purpose of every *mitzvah* of the mouth or deed, however, is to lead to *mitzvot halev* and if it does not lead to this it is a waste. As our teachers taught us 'God desires the heart'."[15]

In *Yesod Mora,* (chapter 8) he further writes: The verse, "For this is your wisdom and your understanding in the eyes of the nations, who will hear all these statutes and say, 'surely this great nation is a wise and understanding people'" taken by Ibn Ezra to imply that there are reasons behind all these statutes which are accessible to the human intellect.[16] In fact, the *taamim* behind many *mitzvot* are clearly stated in the Torah. True, one should not demand a rationale before consenting to practice *mitzvot,* but once an individual is mature and his understanding ripens he should seek the reasons for the commandments. Some reasons may be readily comprehensible, others obscure save to a small few. But intellection over *mitzvot* is not to be regarded, at this stage, as subsidiary to observance. It is perhaps even a part of the observance. Mere observance without a quest for the reason behind practice is insufficient. The quest is crucial to the *neshamah's* ultimate transcendence and nearness to God.

I have chosen, additionally, for translation some of Abraham Ibn Ezra's commentaries on Ecclesiastes as they reflect in a more comprehensive manner the concerns of his philosophic judgments as formulated heretofore. As a personalist, the supreme emphasis in the Hebraic mode of discourse is to know one's own soul. For only as the soul first knows itself will it ultimately know the Creator. But to know itself means first, to perceive its own nature of a soul-making developmental process and secondly, the perception of reason, the power of intellection to enable one to rise to the highest sphere and there receive

its reward by being reunited with the Divine Presence.

The Book of Ecclesiastes, however, adds another significant dimension to self-knowledge by stressing the nature of the self as a locus of obligation and responsibility by virtue of perceiving one's own true nature. In his self-knowledge man becomes aware of his possibilities and these, in turn, imply his responsibilities.

Abraham Ibn Ezra, thus, regarded Ecclesiastes as a profound book of metaphysics. The alleged contradictions inherent in the book, which almost prompted the rabbis of the Talmud to conceal it, are easily resolved in the context of philosophic doctrine. He, likewise, repudiated the assertion by some critics that Ecclesiastes was a collection of several authors with diversified views. The book, he argued, represents a coherent work provided we apply to it the proper philosophical notion, which in this case was the neo-platonic classification of the souls. Thus he demonstrated the enduring value of philosophical exploration even for the proper understanding of biblical texts.

No wonder Maimonides regarded the works of Ibn Ezra superior to any other Jewish scholar. In his "Letter of Instruction to His Son Abraham," he admonished him as follows: "As for you, my faithful son, I exhort you not to pay attention or distract your mind by concentrating on commentaries, treatises and books other than those of Ibn Ezra's, which alone are meaningful and profitable to all who study them with intelligence, understanding and deep insight. They are distinguished from the writings of other authors, for Ibn Ezra was in spirit similar to our patriarch Abraham. It behooves you, therefore, to read all his works, and the symbols he alludes to, with thoughtful reflection concentrating intensively upon his words with clear understanding and lucid insight. For the aforementioned scholar feared no one, flattered no one. He travelled extensively, tarrying one day in one place, the next day in another, frequently engaged in the service of kings.

Alas, if I had only been aware of the many observations made by the aforementioned scholar, Abraham Ibn Ezra, of blessed memory, before I wrote my commentary to the *Mishnah* and the books I called *Mishneh Torah* and *Moreh Nebukhim*, I would have drawn your attention to the esoteric knowledge contained in his treatises and books. I admonish you now not to exercise your rational faculty and precious soul on any other treatise but ours and his, for the latter will endure the span of time, while the other works are worthless and inconsequential."[16]

ABRAHAM IBN EZRA'S INTRODUCTION TO ECCLESIASTES

The highest virtue in life is reason. Its achievement will save one from the nether-world. As the captive longs to return to the land of his birth and be reunited with his family, so the rational soul strives to ascend to the upper reaches of the sphere until it rises to the highest sphere of the living God which is completely devoid of earthly matter. For human bodies are perishable flesh and resemble houses whose foundations are of clay.

This process of ascent can be achieved if the spirit purifies itself and is purged of the defilements of corporeal desires which drag it down to the nether-world. The soul must further take pains to know its own origin and comprehend its own nature,[18] with the help of Wisdom whose "eyes" are undimmed, bringing the far-off, remote places near to us and making night appear like day.[19] The soul will then be prepared to know the truth which will be indelibly impressed upon her and will not disappear even when she separates from the body.

The Lord decreed that the soul makes her appearance here and remain locked in a physical enclosure for an allotted time for her own benefit and welfare. If she endured much anguish during her life span, she will then enjoy everlasting bliss without end. For every activity may be divided into four headings: it is either all good, partially good and partially bad, totally bad, or partially bad and partially good. The first division is a gift of God; the second represents the average life on earth. The remaining two are non-existent, for the Lord God can do only good. Everything in the world is good, as scripture says, "And God saw everything He made and behold it was very good." And if some evil prevailed, it was only on the fringes, which cannot obviate God's abundant goodness.

The root of evil lies in the deficiency of the recipient. For as far as God is concerned, we have no other way of comparing His deeds in the world except by His own handiwork, for, indeed, everything is His handiwork. Thus, for instance, when we behold that the sun, which is one of God's handiworks, will let white garments exposed to its rays remain white while at the same time cause the face of the launderer to turn tan, we must assume that effects vary with the differences in the nature of the recipient. For, in truth, only one form of activity can emanate from one source. Hence changes are due to the specific nature of the objects. By the same token, the thoughts of people are governed by the variety of their physical natures. The changes in the nature of objects are due to motions in the heavenly bodies, the position of the sun and the disposition of the recipients to its influences. Likewise, the events of the sublunar world, its laws, crop production and innumerable objects are governed by the same process.

The Lord, the God of Israel, stirred the spirit of his beloved Solomon to probe significant matters and instruct us in the paths of righteousness. For all of man's work is in vain; it cannot endure. Man can neither create a substance nor annihilate anything until it is reduced to nothingness. All his activity consists only in combining and separating accidents as well as moving about and coming to rest. Hence, man's deeds are vain and empty. The only thing of value is the fear of God. But no one can reach this stage of the fear of the Lord until he ascends the ladder of wisdom and has acquired understanding.[20]

ECCLESIASTES 7:3

Medical men have already indicated that man possesses three souls. One is the vegetative soul; that is to say, just as in the vegetative kingdom (as in grass, plants, and trees) there is a power we call soul, responsible for growth and reproduction, so man possesses a similar power. This soul grows in strength for a specific time. Its main attribute is corporeal desire and it requires the intake of food for its realization.

The second soul is the animal soul. It uses the faculties of the five senses and is responsible for the power of motion, moving animal and man from place to place.

The third soul, which only man possesses, is referred to as "neshamah." This is the faculty of reason that distinguishes between truth and falsehood. The second soul is midway between the other two souls. God endowed man with a rational faculty, which is also referred to as *lev* in order to actualize every soul's potential in due time. He also provided him with *mitzvot* to make it possible to maintain everything in proper proportion . . .

Now, although the three souls are alluded to by one all-embracing name, we shall distinguish the three different powers of the soul by three specific names: *neshamah, ruach, nefesh*. This will avoid undue elaboration on the various qualities associated with each of the three souls. Thus, the term *nefesh* refers to man's desire to eat, to be merry, and indulge in sexual pleasure. The name *ruach* alludes to our sensations that stir feelings for mastery and self-glorification. *Neshamah* denotes our rational faculty. Saadia made a similar classification of the three souls.

It is, moreover, apparent that when the *nefesh* increases in power, the *neshamah* becomes weaker and has no strength to resist the power of the *nefesh,* reinforced as it is by all the other organs of the body. Hence one who overindulges in food and drink can never acquire wisdom. And when *neshamah* and *ruach* get together they overpower *nefesh* and pave the way for a partial opening of the "eyes" of *neshamah* to comprehend the physical but not yet the metaphysical disciplines. The reason for this limitation is due to the power of *ruach* which strives for mastery and gives rise to the sensation of anger. This is then the implication of the verse: "Better is vexation than laughing, for through the sadness of the countenance the heart is made better" (Ecclesiastes 7:3). Sadness of the countenance refers to vexations (cf. "why are you so vexed?" [Gen. 40:7]), and the "heart" alludes to our rational faculty.

Subsequently, when *neshamah* finally prevails over *nefesh* with the help of *ruach,* it becomes necessary for *neshamah* to be preoccupied exclusively with wisdom in order that with the help of the latter, *neshamah* will be able to overcome *ruach* and render her subservient to *neshamah*. This is the meaning of the verse, "Be not rash in thy spirit to be angry; for anger resteth in the bosom of fools" (Ecclesiastes 7:9). Anger resteth with fools forever but with the wise only temporarily and when necessary (cf. "For where there is much wisdom, there is much vexation" [*ibid.,* 1:18];

"neither show thyself overwise" [*ibid.*, 7:16]). For much wisdom increases indignation over the petty vanities of the world and its inhabitants . . .

Thus, the apparent contradictions that appear in the book of Ecclesiastes where the author seems to say one thing in one instance and its opposite another time are only on the surface. The same applies to the Book of Proverbs where the author says: "Do not answer a fool according to his folly" (26:4) and in the following verse: "Answer a fool according to his folly" (26:5). In the Prophets and the Torah, our principal source book, we find similar contradictions, e.g., "Although verily there shall be no poor among you" (Deut. 15:4) and later, "For the poor shall not cease in the land" (*ibid.*, 15:11). In reality they are similar provided we apply to them the proper philosophic notions.[20]

הקדמת אברהם אבן עזרא ז"ל
לספר קהלת

בשם אשר לו הממשלת, אחל לפרש קהלת

אורח חיים למעלה למשכיל למען סור משאול מטה כי כאשר יתאוה
האורח שנשבה לשוב אל ארץ מולדתו להיות עם משפחתו כן תכסוף הרוח
המשכלת להאחז במעלות הגבוהות עד עלותה אל מערכות אלהים חיים
שאינמו שוכני בתי חומר כי הגויות נמשלות לבתים ובעפר יסודם וכענין די
מדרהון עם בשרא לא איתוהי. וזה יהיה אם תתלבן הרוח ותתקדש מטומאות
תאוות הגויות המגואלות המטנפות הקודש להתערב בשאול מטה ותשיב אל
לבה לדעת יסודה ולראות סודה בעיני החכמה שלא תכהינה ותרחוק כקרוב
לפניה והלילה כיום אז תהי נתכנת לדעת קשט אמרי אמת ויהיו מחוקקין
עליה שלא ימחו בהפרדה מעל גויתה כי המכתב מכתב אלהים הוא כי למען
הראותה הובאה הנה על כן נכלאה במסגר עד עת קץ וכל זה להועיל ולהטיב
לה ואם סבלה עמל שנים במספר כן תנוח ותשמח עולמי עדי עד בלי קץ כי כל
מעשה יפרד והיה לארבעה ראשים טוב כולו או טוב רובו ורע בקצתו או רע
כולו או רע רובו וטוב בקצתו והחלק הראשון הוא מנת בני אלהים והחלק
השני הם החיים אשר על פני האדמה והשנים הנשארים נעדרים לא יתכן
המצאם כי לא יעשה ה' אלהים דבר כי אם טוב כי הכל לעולם הוא טוב
וכן כתוב וירא אלהים את כל אשר עשה והנה טוב מאד ואם היה שם רע
היה בקצתו כי בעבור רע מעט אין בדרך החכמה העליונה למנוע טוב רב
ושורש הרע מחסרון המקבל ואם אין לנו יכולת לדמות מעשה אלהים כי אם
אל מעשיו בעבור היות הכל מעשיו הנה ראינו ילבינו הבגדים השטוחים לשמש
ויחשכו פני הכובס והלא הפועל אחד יוצא מפועל אחד לכן ישתנו הפועלים
בעבור השתנות תולדת המקבלים ומחשבות בני אדם משתנות כפי תולדת
גוייה וגוייה והשתנות התולדות בעבור השתנות המערכות העליונות ומקום
השמש והמקבל כחה והמדינות והדתים והמאכלות ומי יוכל לספר אותם וכל
דרך איש זך בעיניו. ויער ה' אלהי ישראל את רוח שלמה ידידו לבאר דברי

חפץ ולהורות הדרך הישרה כי כל מעשה שיעשה נוצר לא יעמוד כי כל
הנבראים ילאו לברוא עצם שהוא שורש או להכחידו עד שיהיה נעדר רק כל
מעשיהם דמות ותמונה ומקרה להפריד מחובר ולחבר נפרד ולניע נח ולהניח
נע על כן מעשה בני אדם תהו וריק כי אם יראת ה' ולא יוכל איש להשיג
אל מעלת יראתו עד עלותו בסולם החכמה ויבנה ויכונן בתבונה.

קהלת ז'

(ג) טוב כעס. כבר בארו חכמי הראיות שיש באדם שלש נפשות האחת
הנפש הצומחת והענין כי כמו שיש במיני הצמחים והדשאים וכל עץ כח קרא
שמו נפש או מה שתרצה שיגדל גישם הצמח ויגביהנו וירחיבנו כן יש באדם
וזאת הנפש מתגברת עד זמן קצוב וזאת הנפש היא המתאוה והצריכה לאכול
והנפש השנית נפש הבהמה והיא בעלת ההרגשות חמשה ובעלת התנודה
ההולכת ממקום למקום וזאת הנפש גם היא באדם ולאדם לבדו נפש שלישית
היא הנקראת נשמה היא המדברת המכרת בין אמת ושקר בעלת חכמה והנפש
השנית היא אמצעית בין שתי הנפשות והאלהים נטע שכל באדם הוא הנקרא
לב למלאת חפץ כל נפש בעתו וגם עזרהו במצות תעמודנה כל דבר על
מתכונתו . . .

ועתה אפשר אותם בדרך קצרה אע"פ שהשלש נפשות נקראות בשם
אחד בעבור התאחדם כי הנשמה תקרא רוח ונפש לכן אשים שמות להם למען
לא אאריך בתואר כל אחת ויהיה השם הנפש המתאוה לאכול ולשמוח וחשק
המשגל נפש ויהיה שם נפש בעלת ההרגשה המבקשת שררה וגדולה רוח ויהיה
שם נפש בעלת החכמה נשמה ג"כ חלקם רבינו סעדיה גאון ז"ל. וידוע כי
בהתגבר הנפש תחלש הנשמה ואין לה כח לעמוד לפניה בעבור היותה גוף
וכל יצריו עוזרים אותה על כן המתעסק באכילה ושתיה לא יחכם לעולם.
ובהתחבר הנשמה עם הרוח תנצחנה הנפש אז תפקחנה מעט עיני הנשמה
להבין חכמות הגויות לכן לא תוכל לדעת החכמות העליונות בעבור כח הרוח
המבקשת שררה והיא המולידה הכעס. והנה זה פירוש טוב כעס משחוק וענין
כי ברוע פנים ייטב לב היא הדאגה כמו מדוע פניכם רעים וענין לב הוא
השכל ואחר שתתגבר הנשמה על הנפש בעזרת הרוח צריכה הנשמה להתעסק
בחכמה שתעזור אותה עד שתנצח הרוח ותהיה תחת ידיה. וזה פירוש אל
תבהל ברוחך לכעוס וענין כי כעס בחיק כסילים ינוח שהוא עמהם לעולם
ולא יזוז מהם ועם החכם לא ימצא כי אם בעתו לצורך וענין כי ברוב חכמה רב

כעס כענין אל תתחכם יותר כי רוב החכמה ירבה כעסו על הבלי העולם
ועל בני העולם.

וכבר הזכרתי בתחלת הספר כי בעבור רע מעט אין חכמה העליונה
למנוע טוב רב וכמו זה בספר משלי שיאמר וקובץ על יד ירבה והוא האמת
ויש מפזר ונוסף עוד הוא המעט וכן יש רשעים שמגיע אליהם כמעשה הצדיקים
אשר תמצא בספר הזה דבר ופעם שנית יראה שיאמר הפך הדבר גם כי תמצא
בספר משלי כמו אל תען כסיל ענה כסיל גם כן בדברי הנביאים ובתורת
אלהינו שהוא העיקר כמו אפס כי לא יהיה בך אביון כי לא יחדל אביון וכלם
אחת.

7. SHEM TOB IBN FALAQUERA

A Thirteenth Century Philosopher of Personalism

EVALUATION

The historian Graetz describes Shem Tob as "a living encyclopaedia of the sciences of his day, trustworthy on any topic on which information may be required."[1] Falaquera's extensive knowledge of every branch of Jewish learning, as well as his unusual familiarity with the works of Plato and Aristotle as expounded by the Arabic commentators, Avicenna and Averroes, earned him the reputation as the most learned Jewish author of his time. A prolific writer, he compiled seventeen works on a variety of subjects, but his chief concern was with philosophy. And philosophy he defines as the science of the soul which takes precedence over all other sciences.[2] Quoting a famous maxim which he ascribes to certain hermits, "Man, know thy soul and thou wilt know thy Creator," Falaquera concludes that the major concern of philosophic speculation is knowledge of one's self, one's essential being, the uniqueness of one's personality.

Very little is known of Shem Tob's early life. He was born around 1225 in one of the provinces on the Franco-Iberian boundary.[3] A member of one of the city's distinguished Jewish families, he was very likely educated in accordance with the standards of well-to-do Spanish Jews of the era who were trained in science, philosophy, and literature, at the same time that they cultivated rabbinic studies. Certainly the numerous citations in his works of both Arabic and Jewish sources indicate his pervasive knowledge of both cultures. In addition, he was endowed with a poetic, sensitive soul and was a prolific writer of verse.

It appears that he never married[4] and never occupied any public position. He derived some income from his patrimony. Steinschneider[5] maintains that he practiced medicine, although he does not seem to have great esteem for the physicians of his day.[6] Like most of his colleagues, he wandered from place place, leading a hazardous existence but filled with a mission to inspire love for learning and zeal for study. For him study and knowledge were not simply means to attain earthly goods but ultimate ends in themselves. In one of his early works, he writes: "Of what value are the good things of this world compared with the soul's satisfaction that comes from the search after truth?"[7]

It is, indeed, ironic that he penned those words in the thirteenth century which is decribed by many historians as the darkest period in history. It was a century that saw the establishment of the Inquisition, the persecution of dissenting minorities, the enslavement of the intellect and the tyranny of the Roman Church over creative thought and free research.[8]

In the Jewish community, however, the thirteenth century was marked by intellectual activity even among the masses. The cultural interest centered around talmudic research and the study of philosophy initiated by the great controversy over the writings of Maimonides.

Shem Tob was one of the outstanding exponents of Maimonidean thought and the unrelenting defender of the study of philosophy.[9] His commentary on Maimonides' *Guide* under the title *Moreh ha-Moreh* reveals his wide scholarship. By comparing parallel passages from Arabic expositors, especially Averroes, with the Maimonidean text, he sought to elucidate the true meaning of *The Guide*. His translation of Ibn Gabirol's *Fons Vitae* into Hebrew made it possible in 1846 for Solomon Munk, the Jewish orientalist, to reclaim the work for Judaism.

While Shem Tob was not a trail-blazer in the sense of projecting original schemes of philosophical notions, he set for himself a three-fold task which served to break through the barriers the dark ages of medievalism sought to impose on Jewry. In the first place, he championed the rationalism of Maimonides and defended the cause of the philosophers as essential to true religion. Hostility toward philosophy comes from ignorance of the Jewish heritage, he argued. Secondly, he defined philosophy in his chief philosophic treatise *Sefer ha-Nefesh,* as the discipline concerned with the study and knowledge of one's soul. In the tradition of Jewish personalism he, thus, underscored the organized principle of life in the Hebraic world scheme.

This notion of philosophy gave rise to his third challenge, which was to stir in others a zeal for study and learning[10] as a discipline for the soul. Knowledge and intellectual excellence, according to personalistic doctrine, is more than a mere search for truth. It is a means of ecstatic union of the human spirit with the divine spirit. Religious observances, designed as a discipline to curb our animal impulses, pave the way for our intellect and pure spirit to conceptualize and contemplate the ultimate truths of philosophy unhampered. This, in turn, leads to an attainment of human perfection and self-realization and ultimate union with the Infinite. We can now appreciate Falaquera's passion for intellectual activity and for study and speculation.

What follows is my translation of Shem Tob's introduction to his *Sefer ha-Nefesh* which was written as a compendium on medieval psychology.

INTRODUCTION TO *SEFER HA-NEFESH*

Said Shem Tob ben Joseph ibn Falaquera:

I deemed it appropriate to write a brief treatise on the science of the soul drawing from the works of the latest Arabic philosophers,[11] who rationalized by means of investigation and research. While this is to be a short study it will embrace most of what they had to say about the science of the soul and the authentic conclusions they reached through philosophic investigation. Although I had already recorded at length all these notions in another work I wrote on the *Opinions of the Philosophers*,[12] I saw fit to write this treatise in order that it may serve me as a review manual that I might refer to repeatedly.[13] For it is, indeed, proper for everyone who seeks knowledge, that he become thoroughly conversant with this particular science which leads to an apprehension of one's essential being and, in turn, to the attainment of the ultimate goal of knowing one's Creator, blessed be He.

Philosophers have maintained that all sciences are worthwhile and rewarding, but that some are more rewarding than others and that the science of the soul takes precedence over all other disciplines in the category of values. A discipline is worthwhile when its notions are authentic like the science of mathematics, or its postulates have value like the science of astronomy. But a knowledge of the soul is superior to both.

The scholars have also asserted that the mark of perfection is twofold: to love knowledge with utmost devotion and to choose the purest of activities with meaningful intentions. Hence, when man knows himself he attains perfect knowledge. For perfect knowledge of a substance consists in the apprehension of its form, as this constitutes the true knowledge of its essential being.

Moreover, the philosophers said that he who understands his soul knows his Creator. And, by the same token, one who is ignorant in the science of his soul is surely devoid of any knowledge of his Creator.[14] How, then, can one have faith in man who has achieved wisdom in all other branches of knowledge but is ignorant of the science of his soul!

They [the philosophers] further maintained that the confused who forget God, blessed be He, actually forget their souls as it is written in the scrolls of the hermits, "Man, know thy soul and thou wilt know thy Creator." This is such a true maxim! For so many properties are attributed to the faculties of the soul. Even the mysterious and theological disciplines may be explained through psychological studies. For this reason, they said, that knowledge of the soul is a prelude to knowledge of the Deity and that the former constitutes the supreme discipline next to the science of the Deity [theology].

I have divided this treatise into twenty chapters as follows: 1. Proof for the existence of the soul. 2. Air as the bearer of the medium for the powers of the soul. 3. A definition of the soul. 4. The necessary elements of the soul's faculties. 5. The nutritive faculty. 6. The power of sensation. 7. The sense of sight. 8. The sense of hearing. 9. The sense of smell. 10. The sense of taste. 11. The sense of touch. 12. The faculty of common sense (an internal sense—*sensus communis*). 13. The faculty of imagination. 14. The rational faculty. 15. The unique properties of the rational faculty. 16. The faculty of memory. 17. The vital power. 18. A summary of the overall faculties of the soul. 19. Ancient theories of the soul. 20. The influence of the active intellect upon the soul.[15]

הקדמת המחבר ספר הנפש
מרבי שם טוב פלקיירה זלה"ה

אמר שם טוב בר' יוסף ז"ל בן פלקירה. ראיתי לחבר ספר קטן בחכמת
הנפש, ואחברהו מספרי הפילוסופים האחרונים המדברים ע"ד החקירה והחפוש,
ויהיה דברי בו בקצרה, ויהיה כולל רוב מה שאמרו בחכמת הנפש, ומה
שהסכימו עליו שהוא אמת מצד החקירה, ואף עפ"י שכבר כתבתי כל אלה
הענינים באריכות בספר שחברתי בדעות הפילוסופים, ראיתי לחבר זה הספר
בעבור שיהיה לי ספר זכרון, אעיין בו תמיד, כי כן ראוי לעשות כל מבקש
החכמה שישים זאת החכמה נכח עיני לבו כי בה ידע עצמו וממנה יגיע אל
התכלית האחרון שהוא ידיעת בוראו יתברך. ואמרו החכמים כי כל חכמה
מפוארה ומעולה אלא שמקצת החכמות מעולות ממקצתן, וחכמת הנפש קודמת
לשאר החכמות במיני העילוי כולם. והחכמה תהיה מעולה בהיות ענינה
אמיתים (כחכמת המספר) או בהיות מונחה מעולה כחכמת הכוכבים, וחכמת
הנפש נכבדת משניהם יחדיו. ואמרו כי ראשית המעלות שנים, אהבת החכמה
באמונות, ובחירת הזך מהמעשים בכוונות. ובידיעת האדם נפשו תהיה בו
ידיעתו שלמה. כי השלמה שבידיעת הדבר היא ידיעת צורתו ובידיעת צורתו
ידע מה הוא עצמו. ואמרו כי מי שידע נפשו ידע בוראו. וכל מי שהוא סכל
בידיעת נפשו כ"ש שהוא סכל בידיעת בוראו. ואיך יאמן באדם שהוא חכם
בזולתו והוא סכל בנפשו. ואמרו כי התועים שכחו האלהי ית' והשכיחם
נפשותיהם. והיה כתוב בהיכל הפרושים דע נפשך בן אדם ותדע בוראך. וזה
ענין אמיתי כי כמה דברים יוחסו לכחות הנפש יתבאר בו החכמה שהם
מרוחקים מהשכל כ"ש מהאלהי ית' ע"כ אמרו כי ידיעת הנפש קודמת לידיעת
האלהי ית'. ושהיא המעולה שבידיעות אחר השי"ת (וראיתי לחלק זה הספר
לעשרים פרקים).

8. HILLEL BEN SHMUEL

The Individual Soul's Immortal Core

EVALUATION

The first Jewish philosopher to write a book dealing exclusively with psychology is Hillel ben Shmuel of Verona (1220-1295). His book, *Tagmule ha-Nefesh* (The Rewards of the Soul), was written in order to obviate any wrong conception of the soul. Since the soul constitutes the very essence of man, any erroneous conception of man's essence might lead to false notions about the universe and even God Himself.[1] For the key to an understanding of the ultimate reality of existence lies in the study of the nature and destiny of man. The accent in Jewish thought is on Personalism. It is on the level of human experience that we respond to the eternal challenge of the unknown. It is from the perspective of man's frame of reference[2] that a determination is made whether the response is of an analytical or a poetic, synoptic nature. The human condition, the existential situation, sets in motion relationships with the unknown, the phenomenal world and society.

Hillel ben Shmuel was born in Verona, Italy, in 1220. In Italy during the 13th century, the Jews fared better economically and politically than in some other countries, but culturally the 13th century was comparatively inferior to others. Hillel ben Shmuel was the first devotee of Jewish learning and philosophy in Italy in the middle of the century. In his youth, he

went to Spain to study the Talmud at the academy of Jonah
Gerundi at Barcelona, and philosophy and science with other
masters. Upon his return to his native country, he settled in
Ferra and Forli where he was engaged in the practice of
medicine.

A strong admirer of Maimonides, he undertook to defend
him against the attacks of his opponents and proposed a con-
ference of scholars to judge the works and philosophy of the
great master. He wrote a commentary on Maimonides' twenty-
five propositions.

His knowledge of Latin gave him access to the writings
of the scholastics. He translated many of their works as well
as several medical treatises into Hebrew, among them a book
of surgery. He also translated the neo-Platonic *Liber de Causis*
and made extensive use of many other philosophic and scientific
books in Latin. Moreover, it was his knowledge of Latin that
enabled him to make use of the refutation of Averroes by
Thomas Aquinas.

His title as a Jewish philosopher rests on his main philosophic work *Tagmule ha-Nefesh*[3] which treats of man's essential
being, the soul, as a developmental, functional process destined
to life everlasting. The book is chiefly a refutation of Averroe's
theory of the soul and intellect, known as the *unitas intellectus.*
The implications of this scheme, according to Hillel, would
undermine the central personalistic position of Jewish philosophy
with its emphasis on the individual soul's immortal core.

Let me elucidate. Aristotle in his exposition of the
rational soul divides the psyche into a "passive intellect" which
is the power of knowing and becoming all universals, and the
"active intellect" which makes all things, a kind of quality

(*hexis*), like light. And it is this *nous* which is "separable, impassible, unmixed since it is in its essential nature activity" (*De Anima* Bk. III: 5, 430ª).[4] But where is that activity located? If knowing is like an illumination by an intelligible light, then, are we not back to a Platonic conception of the soul? The problem is that Aristotle's statement on the subject is ambiguous. He does not pursue the point. After a brief single paragraph, he goes on in a thoroughly naturalistic view as before.

Aristotle's pupil, Theophrastas, maintained that the so-called "active intellect" is really "in the psyche" part of the human *nous*, one of the human functions of our life.

Alexander of Aphrodisius, the Hellenic commentator, held that it is a cosmic *nous*, an eternal activity in the world, God Himself. This Platonizing interpretation was adopted by St. Augustine.

The Arabic commentator of the twelfth century Spain, Averroes, posited the unity of the intellect—*Unitas Intellectus*—which construed both the passive and active intellect as a kind of realm of truth in which men participate. Intellect is the same for all men. It is not a personal human activity but a universal faculty which actualizes itself in men as knowledge. But man does not think himself at all. Only "intellect" ever thinks in us. We simply possess a "cogitative soul" or imagination to serve as the instrument of this single rational intellect of all mankind.

But what about the individuality of particular souls? Surely the Averroeistic doctrine of the Universal Intellect threatened to undermine one of the fundamental principles of religion, namely, the individual soul's immortal core.[5] In the

Averroeistic scheme, when the passive power of our *phantasia* reaches the highest degree of perfection it, then, becomes active and unites with the Universal Intellect after the death of the individual. There is no individual immortality since there is no individual intellect. But Averroes was regarded as the great interpreter of Aristotle and the former's authority was excelled only by the latter. How, then, reconcile his doctrine without making a breach with religion?[6]

The first book dealing exclusively with this subject is *Tagmule ha-Nefesh* by Hillel ben Shmuel. The book consists of two parts. The first deals with the philosophical aspect of the problem of the soul, such as its existence, essence, indivisibility and function. In the second part, he takes up the theological problem of the soul's reward and punishment. Defining the soul as an emanated formal substance which subsists through its own perfection and occupies the fourth place in the order of spiritual beings, namely, God, the Separate Intelligences, the Active Intellect and the Soul,[7] he comes to the crucial question of the relation of the soul to the Active Intellect and the body, as well as the activity and immortality of the human intellect, the higher part of the soul.

Unlike Averroes, who held that the intellect is neither a part of the soul nor its form, Hillel asserts that the human active intellect is part of the soul and its very form emanates from one universal soul in a descending series. The objection that forms cannot come from other forms for, then, it would have to proceed by way of genesis and dissolution, a process belonging only to matter and not to form, Hillel discounts as invalid. He argues that only the action of body upon body which is by contact is subject to a process of genesis and dissolution. But forms, like other Intelligences, come from the one previous to it by way of emanation, which applies also to human individual souls emanating from one universal soul.[8] Averroes' objection to the temporal origin of the soul does not apply to the process of emanation. This rational part of every human soul, then, remains after death and is subject to reward and punishment.

After projecting the possibility of the soul as a form of the body he, then, proceeds to assert that the soul contains powers which are independent of the body.[9] These potential powers of the material intellect[10] constitute a component of the individual soul and are actualized when acted upon by the universal intellect, setting in motion the process of conceptualization.[11] Whether in a neo-platonic or Aristotelian version, the soul of man is, thus, considered a special type of active form emanating from the universal soul, whose destiny is determined by the laws corresponding to its essence. Accordingly, its immortality is dependent upon the level of knowledge reached.

In a purely personalistic tradition, Hillel establishes his premises which contribute to the solution of a crucial philosophical problem. In the first place, he projects the uniqueness of man's position in the sublunar world[12] by virtue of his soul, which is a special type of active form proceeding from form by way of emanation similar to the celestial separate Intelligences. In the sublunar world only man possesses the special form capable of conceptualization by the supra-personal substance of the Active Intellect. Such a form is not limited by time or place. It is potentially divine.

Then, again, underscoring the personalistic emphasis on the development of man's capacities to receive the form, Hillel is able to strike a compromise between the Averroistic notion of one universal soul and its individualization in men, by virtue of considering only the *potential intellect* a component of the individual soul. The supra-personal character of the active intellect, is comparable to the light of the sun with its division into many rays whose effectiveness depends upon the multiplicity of its receiving objects and the disposition of those objects. In the philosophic scheme of personalism, the capacity to receive and respond determines the effectiveness of the benefaction vouchsafed by the dispenser.[13]

In a deeper sense, the potential aspect of man's intellect, underscored in personalism, is the key to an understanding of one of the basic theologic — philosophical problems agitating medieval thinkers, namely, the reconciliation of natural reason with divine revelation.[14] In a personalistic context, natural reason is an inclination, a capacity, an openness in man's intellectual faculty to respond to the revelatory process that makes for self-realization and actualization by appropriating doctrinal beliefs as forms of our religious consciousness. Its merit lies not at the opposite pole in a polarity of two distinct contradictory substances but as an element of one substance—one is actuality; the other potentiality striving toward actuality.

What follows is my translation of Hillel's introduction to *Tagmule ha-Nefesh.*

Tagmule ha-Nefesh: "THE REWARDS OF THE SOUL"

The author Hillel, son of the saintly R. Shmuel, son of the Gaon R. Eliezer of Verona, said: It is generally acknowledged among all men of science that the most precious possession of man is the soul, and its well-being constitutes the ultimate purpose of man's existence. And yet, the number of those who are impervious to the study of the origin and the destiny of the soul is constantly increasing over those who would take pains to engage in this discipline almost to the point of one hundred to one. And even the few who do undertake to investigate this important subject are unable to arrive at the truth. For the matter itself is difficult and requires long preparations and preliminary knowledge. Then, again, the natural indolence of man when it comes to study, coupled with the general vicissitudes of life and its short duration, completely account for the lack of true knowledge among men.

These considerations induced me, for the sake of Heaven, to write a small, comprehensive treatise that will embrace in concise form the various notions necessary to apprehend the illuminations of the soul with which the Almighty has endowed us. The work of this treatise although quantitatively small was exceedingly difficult for me, due to my limited intelligence, lack of imagination and subtlety respecting the underlying principles. I, therefore, set out to collect a variety of notions scattered among the extensive works of the philosophers, arranging them and expounding upon them in such a concise and lucid manner so that their investigation will not be too cumbersome and discourage those in search of wisdom.

The purpose I sought in this enterprise is the knowledge of truth for such knowledge has only one end and that is that its knowledge is truth.[15] It is similar to the statement of the rabbis that the reward of the *mitzvah* is the *mitzvah*. Although some interpret this statement to mean that the performance of one *mitzvah* will inevitably lead to the performance of another *mitzvah*, both inferences are correct and convey the same meaning.

For this reason, I directed my attention in this work to explain the existence of the soul, its nature and reward. Apprehending the truth of this discipline, we shall then arrive at the truth of ultimate reality. For the soul is that which makes man man, and puts us in the category of humanity.

Hence we should not forget our formative constituent nature, namely, the essence of our being. Nor should we neglect to know the nature of that which makes us intelligent beings, else we don't deserve the name of intelligent or even human beings but are likened unto cattle and beast. Compare the admonition of the Psalmist "Be ye not like the horse or like the mule, who hath no understanding . . ." (Ps. 32:9).

Another important reason for the study of the nature of the soul, known otherwise as the rational faculty, is that any erroneous notions in this matter lead to more serious mistakes in other areas of knowledge and belief, as I shall explain presently. Suppose an ordinary man who calls himself pious assumes that the soul after leaving the body will be subject to corporeal reward and punishment, as would appear from a hasty, nimble, confused and literal rendering of Biblical and Talmudic passages he would, by the same token, be led to imagine that the soul is also corporeal. This he would derive from the fact that any object capable of being acted upon by a corporeal object is itself corporeal. If, then, the soul after departing is subject to corporeal retribution, it must also be corporeal.

Now, this notion may not in itself be so harmful if not for the dreadful consequences one may draw from it regarding other doctrinal beliefs. For, as soon as we apprehend the soul to be of some corporeal nature either of a very thin or luminous substance shining like the sun, we are led inevitably to believe that the celestial world must have bodies and definite places, since it is believed that the soul comes from on-high. This apprehension leads immediately to the assumption that the angels are corporeal. Now, since angels are emanations from the Divine splendor, as the masses maintain, in keeping with a Rabbinic interpretation of the verse in Psalms, "He covereth himself with light as with a garment"

(104:2) and, inasmuch, as it is well known that the first emanation is generally similar to the emanator, the conclusion is inevitable that God too is body. Once we make such a deduction, you can readily see what happens: we have destroyed the soul, . . . and repudiated the fundamentals of our faith.

Accordingly, I sought to present in this treatise sufficient material for those searching for the truth as you will presently see, and divided the book into two parts. In the first part, I expound upon several aspects relating to the soul. In this part I have included a special significant chapter designed to strengthen our sacred faith. In the other chapters of the first part I discuss also briefly the three kinds of intellect and the soul's union with the active intellect.

The second part treats of the soul's reward and punishment after its parting from the body. I shall support my assumptions with Biblical and Talmudic references, and attempt to resolve what may appear to the ignorant at the outset apparent contradictions. I, therefore, called this treatise *Tagmule ha-Nefesh,* and exhort every intelligent person not to read the book hastily but with penetrating deliberation, stripped of any trace of envy. Should he discover some mistakes, I hope that, for the sake of the Almighty, he will investigate them thoroughly and point them out to me and I promise to accept his authoritative judgment as a student accepts the advice of his teacher. May the Lord help me in this task!

The first part contains seven sections. The first section proves the existence of the soul.[16] The second proves that the soul is a substance, not a corporeal entity, not a property, not an accident.[17] In the third section I shall prove that the soul is not subject to any form of motion, nor divisible, nor unchangeable in any form.[18] The fourth will deal with a definition of the soul.[19] The fifth raises the question whether there are in essence a multiplicity or unity of souls in which I shall prove conclusively its unity.[20] The sixth section proves the existence of three kinds of intellect and points out the manner in which the rational part of the soul unites with the active intellect.[21] The seventh section deals with the relation of our material intellect to the rest of the human soul, refuting the contrary assertions of those (like Averroes) who say that that the possible intellect is not the form of the soul nor part of the soul.[22]

The second part of the book contains three sections. In the first section, I discuss the various forms of reward and punishment; whether they are corporeal or spiritual. I conclude that they must be devoid of corporeal nature which I demonstrate from the point of view of the justice of God and from a knowledge of the science of nature.[23] The second section deals with the nature of spiritual reward and punishment. In the third section, I interpret the various statements of the rabbis which on the surface would ascribe corporeality to reward and punishment. But, as I shall show, this is not the case.[24]

ספר תגמולי הנפש

אמר המחבר הלל בן החסיד הרב ר' שמואל בן הגאון ר' אליעזר
מוירונא זצ"ל. עם היות נודע אצל כל אנשי החכמה כי הקנין המפואר שימצא
במין האנושי הוא הנפש והצלחתה והוא התכלית האחרון לאדם במציאתו
ועם כל זה רבו הבלתי משגיחים לדעת מה היא מה ראשיתה ומה אחריתה
על המשגיחים בכך עד שכמעט לא יגיעו לסכום מספר אחד למאה מחמת
מיעוטם והקצת ההוא מן המשגיחים לא יכלו לעמוד על אמיתת זה הענין
הנכבד עם התחבר להיותו עמוק בעצמו ואורך ההוצעות והקדמות הצריכות
ללכת לפניו עם עצלות הלימוד ורוב תכופות מקרי הזמן וקוצר החיים שכל
אלה הם סבות גדולות על התמעט ידיעות החכמות בדור האנושי. אלה הענינים
העירו את רוחי לטרוח לשם שמים שאעשה חיבור אחד קטן כללי מקבל
בקצרה הדברים המוכרחים לדעת מאורות הנפש לכל אשר נגע אלהים בלבו,
וזאת המלאכה מזה החיבור גם אם היא קטנות השיעור היא עלי גדולה
לחולשת שכלי ומיעט ציורי וחוזק ראשיותה ופניתי אני לאסוף נפזרי
הדברים האלה מתוך ספרי הפילוסופים שהם גדולים ורחבי ידים וסדרתים
ופירשתים בקצרה בפירוש מבואר כדי שלא יכבד עיונם על מבקשי החכמה
ויזנחום ולא בקשתי בזה אלא התועלת שתושג במציאות זאת התכלית והוא
ידיעת האמת לבד שאין לידיעת האמת זולת תכלית אחת לבד והוא לדעת
שהוא אמת, וזה דומה קצת למה שאמרו חז"ל שכר מצוה מצוה ואע"פ שהפי'
שהקב"ה מביא לידו מצוה אחרת שניהם בנעימים והכל שב אל ענין אחד
אצל מי שיבין אותו הפי', ולכן סבותי אל לבי בזה החיבור לבאר מציאות
הנפש וענינה ותגמולי' עד שנעמוד על אמתתה ואז ישלם לנו מציאות זה
התכלית באמת מזה המין של החכמה כשנדע שהיא אמת, וזה בעבור היות שהנפש
היא הדבר שבעבורה נהי' האיש איש וכי נמצא במציאות אנושית א"כ אין
ראוי שננשכח אנחנו מה שעשתה אנחנו ר"ל מציאות עצמנו, גם אין ראוי
שנתיאש מהשכיל אותו הדבר בעצמו שעשאנו משכילים שאם נעשה כן לא
נהיו משכילים ולא אפילו אנשים אמנם נהי' על מדריגות הבהמית ושאר
בע"ח וע"ז הזהיר הנביא לא תהי' כסוס כפרד אין הבן וכו'. עוד יש בזה

העיון תועלת אחרת גדולה מאד והיא שאפשר כי בהחל האדם לחשוב בעניני
הנפש המדברת והיא המשכלת רציאנעל בלע"ז מחשבות רעות ונפסדות יגיע
מהם אל מחשבה אחרת יותר רעה כמו שאומר עתה לך. תציע היות אחד
מהמון ישראל המתדמה כחסיד ידמה בלבבו כי הנפש אחרי הפרדה מן הגוף
ישיגה ענינים גופיים במיני שלומיה ותגמולין כמו יראה לנו בשלוח ובהעברה
ובהבהלה מפשוטי הפסוקים ופשטי ההגדות שבתלמוד ידמה ג"כ עם הדמיון
דמיון אחר ויחשוב שהנפש הוא גוף ויגזור כך הואיל שכל מקבל התפעלות
גופיי הוא גוף בהכרח והנפש מקבלת אחר הפרדה התפעלות גופיית כלומר
עונשים גופיים א"כ היא גוף והי' זאת המחשבה אעפ"י שאינה כ"כ רבת
ההיזק מצד עצמה היא רבת ההיזק מצד מה שאפשר לה להמשך אחרי'
שאר אמונות נפסדות מאבידות בעבור כי תיכף ציירו בציורו השכלי שהנפש היא
גוף יהי' מה שיהי' או דק מאוד או מאיר ומזהיר כשמש לאלתר יביאהו ההכרח
לצייר שיש למעלה בעולם העליון גופים ומקומות מוגבלים עם כל מה שהתקבל
אצל כל אדם שהנפש ניתנה מלמעלה. ובציורו שיש בעולם העליון גופים
לאלתר יביאהו זה הציור שהמלאכים גופים ועם היות אצלו המלאכים גופים
וכבר התאמת אצל ההמון שהמלאכים הם אצולם מהוד הש"י ב"ה כמו
שדרשו חז"ל על פסוק עוטה אור כשלמה וגו' וידוע שהמאציל לא יאציל
ראשונה אלא בדומה לו מזה יגזור שהוא ית"ש ח"ו הוא ג"כ גוף ותיכף הגיעו
לזו הנקודה הגיע לשריפת נשמה וגוף אבד וכפר בעיקר ראה מה קרה לזה.
לכן השתדלתי להודיע בחיבורי זה מה שיספיק למבקש האמת כמו שתראה
וחלקתיו לשני חלקים. בחלק הא' אבאר שבעה ענינים בנפש ובכלל זה החלק
יכנס מאמר אחד נכבד על אודות חיזוק האמונה הקדושה. אמנם ממעלתו
יחדתי לו שער בפ"ע ובזה החלק הא' אבאר ג"כ בקצרה שלשה מיני השכלים
וענין התדבקות הנפש בשכל הפועל. ובחלק ב' אבאר אמת תגמולי הנפש
העתידה לה ב בשכר ועונש אחרי הפרדה מן הגוף ושם אחזק דברי מן המקרא
ומן התלמוד ואפשר כמה דברים שנראים בהתחלת ההבטה אל בלתי מבין
שנראים כסותרין זה העניין שכוונתי אליו. ובכן תשלים לי הכוונה בחיבור
זה וקראתיו בשם מאמר תגמולי הנפש וכל איש משכיל שיקרא בו אני משביע
בנפשו שלא יעבור עליו בשילוח רק יתבונן בו במתון התבוננות מופשטות
מתאוה ומקנאה ואח"כ אם יראה בו שגיאות ידקדק בהם ויורני האמת לשם
שמים ואני מעכשיו התקבלתי אדנות חכמות קבלת תלמיד מרבו וד' אלהים
יעזור לי.

ציוני החלק הא' בם שבעה. א', אודיע שהנפש נמצאת. ב', אודיע שהיא
עצם בלתי גוף, בלתי חומר, בלתי סגולה, בלתי מקרה. ג', אודיע שהיא בלתי
מתנועעת בשום אחד ממיני התנועות ושהיא בלתי נחלקת ושהיא בלתי
משתנת בשום אחד ממיני השינוים. ד', אודיע מה היא על דרך התרת הגדר
ואתן את גדרה. ה', אודיע אם היא אחת במספר העצם או רבות ואוכיח
לפי שום אופן שהיא אחת. ו', מדרגת השכל ואומר שהם ג' ואבאר מציאותם
במופתים ואראה איך השכל שהוא חלק א' מהנפש יש לו באחרית התאחדות
בשכל הפועל וזה אזכירו מאוד. ז', אודיע איך השכל שבנו חלק מהנפש
האנושית הנושעת ואסתור דברי האומרים שאינו נפש ולא חלק מנפש.

ציוני החלק הב' הם ג'. בראשון אתוכח על מיני תגמולי הנפש
ועונשי' אם הם גופים חומריים או לא ואוכיח שמן הנמנע הוא היותם גופים
חומרם. וזה אראה מצד הצדק האלהי ומדרך אופני חכמת הטבעית. ב', אודיע
מה המה באמת כלומר השכרים והעונשים ובזה עוד יכנס מיני החלוקים
שחלקתי כל דברי חז"ל שנראה משטח דבריהם שתגמולי הנפש המה חומריים
גופים ואין הדבר כן אלא הפירוש הוא כמו שאראה שם.

IV

A KEY TO AN UNDERSTANDING OF THE
MAJOR PHILOSOPHERS

A basic assumption of this treatise is that the minor Jewish philosophers are the key to an understanding of the major Jewish philosophers. Once we have an insight into the conceptual structure of the minor philosophers, the works of the major philosophers take on a new perspective reflecting the true essence of an independent Jewish philosophic scheme. While the major philosophers incorporated into their ideological constructs other systems and permitted the intrusion of copious quotations from a variety of external sources — for this reason they are referred to as major philosophers—in a personalistic framework, they applied them to their own central thesis of *Torat ha-Nefesh,* the study of man. The ten treatises of Saadia's *Emunot v'Deot,* or the three books of Maimonides' *Moreh Nebukhim,* or the four treatises of Crescas' *Or Hashem* are not unconnected, disjointed compendiums of science, metaphysics, theology, ethics, logic and epistemology, compiled in an eclectic, incoherent manner from extraneous disciplines to demonstrate that Jews could also philosophize. No wonder that modern philosophical scholarship, such as the school of the *Wissenschaft des Judentums* centered primarily on discovering the sources for the modes of discourse of our classical philosophers. In our context, however, the major thrust of Jewish scholarship focuses on the question how the neo-platonic, Kalamistic or Aristotelian categories, which our philosophers incorporated into their scheme, helped to project the authentic, central thesis of Jewish philosophy.

Accordingly, the various treatises of the works of the major philosophers are not unmotivated independent studies of philosophic themes collected haphazardly into a book. They reflect rather a coherent area of investigation revolving around an all-illuminating core of personalism. Our philosophers took the neo-platonic, Kalamistic or Aristotelian categories and applied them not to the latter's physics, metaphysics or logic but to their own leitmotif. The works of our major philosophers should be studied, therefore, with a view of determining the relevance of each treatise of the book to the basic core that is uniquely Hebraic.

a. SAADIA

It is, indeed, significant that the works of the major philosophers commence with reference to the primacy of man as a point of departure for philosophic inquiry. Saadia (892-942) in the first passage of his introductory treatise of *Emunot v'Deot* says: "Blessed be God, the God of Israel . . . who verifies with certainty unto rational beings the existence of their souls . . ."[1]

Preoccupation with the existence of one's soul by which to attain truth, constitutes God's greatest challenge to man and is projected by Saadia as the major thesis of his philosophic exposition. Thus, the fourth, fifth and sixth treatises of *Emunot v'Deot,* dealing with the nature of man are the leitmotif of the whole book and every other treatise should be regarded as a concomitant to his doctrine of man. The fourth treatise projects the nature of man as central in the universe because of his rational constitution. "By means of this wisdom he is able to retain all the events of the past and forsee many of the eventualities of the future, and achieve the subjugation of the animals so as to make them till the soil for him and transport to him its harvest. By means of it, too, he succeeds in extracting water from the depths of the earth to the point where it flows on its surface. Nay, he makes himself water-wheels by means of which the soil is automatically watered. By dint of this wisdom he is furthermore able to build the most exquisite dwellings, wear the choicest garments, and prepare the most delicious foods. By means of it he becomes capable also of leading hosts and armies and of exercising governmental authority in such a way that men will allow themselves to be bound and ruled thereby. By means of it, moreover, he attains to the knowledge of the disposition of the heavenly spheres and the course of the stars and the measurements of their masses and their distances and all the rest of their attributes. Should anyone, however, imagine that there exists some other being outside of man that is endowed with such superior qualities, then let him show us these qualities or even some of them in another creature. Such a being, however, he will never discover. Although man is not the largest of the creatures, by virtue of his soul he encompasses the entire universe."[2]

The fifth treatise stresses the nature of man as a potential for good or evil. "The activities of man leave their traces upon their souls, rendering them pure or sullied. Thus, Scripture says, apropos of (the effect of) sin: 'Then he shall bear his iniquity' (Lev. 5:1) . . . 'Its inquity shall rest on that soul' " (Num. 15:31).[3] Theodicy "as a testing of the soul by God provided He knows that they will be able to endure it," and Repentance are included in this treatise as motivations for authenticating one's potentialities.

The sixth treatise delineates the structure of the soul as the essence of man. After discussing three categories of misconceptions about the nature of the soul — the insubstantiality, corporeality and pluralistic nature of the soul,[4] Saadia proceeded to define the soul as a unique luminous substance purer and simpler than the celestial spheres. It is unique because it alone is endowed with intellect. It is simpler than the heavenly bodies which are not endowed with reason.[5] It is created after the formation of the body and is linked to the body which serves as an instrument for its development. Although a unified transparent substance, the soul has three main faculties, the vegetative, the affective and the intellectual. The Bible itself distinguishes these faculties by referring to the lowest faculty as *nefesh,* to the middle faculty as *ruah* and to the intellectual faculty as *neshamah.* By virtue of its uniqueness it is designated as *yehida* and insofar as it is immortal it is called *haya* (*Emunot,* 6, 3).

According to most scholars, Saadia's definition of the soul appears to mediate between Plato who considered the soul as an independent entity, and approaching the Aristotelian concept of the soul as an entelechy of the body, inasmuch as he placed it in a relationship with the body.[6]

The fact, however, is that Saadia's notion of the soul as an independent substance may be identified with the personalistic concept of a functional substantialism which refers to the ultimate state of the soul's development, when it takes on a content of its own. Surely this is the case with the intellectual faculty which Saadia claims cognizes through itself, by virtue of its own being. Cognition cannot be mediated by the body. For is not a blind man able to see in his dreams, argues Saadia, although he is deprived of the visual organ?[7]

Clearly, these three treatises constitute the conceptual framework of Saadia's classical work. The treatises preceeding them are an extention of his exposition on the nature of man. The treatises following them are concomitants of his thesis on the destiny of man. Let me elucidate.

The prolegomena is an epistemological exposition delineating man's quest for the truth of self-authentication. There are three sources of knowledge by which we can cognize the truth — sense experience, intuitive knowledge and derivative rational knowledge. Revelation and tradition confirm the independent findings of the other three sources of knowledge.[8] Reason, Saadia further argues, will help "the believer who blindly relies on tradition (to) turn into one basing his belief on speculation and understanding. . . . In this way the innermost thoughts of a man will be purified and brought into conformity with his outward behaviour; his prayer will be sincere as there will be enshrined in his heart an inner voice rebuking and summoning him to right conduct, as the prophet says, 'Thy words have I laid up in my heart, that I might not sin against Thee' " (Ps. 119:11).[9]

The treatise on Creation is not merely a scientific exposition but the backdrop to a study of man as a universe in miniature. The world in its relationship to its Creator is compared to that of man's soul and body. In his commentary to *Sefer Yezirah*,[10] he elaborates on the relationship by stating that just as God is distinguished from the world so is the soul distinct from the body. Just as God is called the Life of the World (Daniel, 12, 7) because He harmonizes all its parts, so the soul harmonizes the parts of the body. Just as God controls the world by means of His Will, so the intellectual faculty of man controls the body. Just as God outlives His creatures and is higher than anything else in the world although He is present in all things, so the rational faculty of the soul is higher and does not perish when the body does.[11]

The treatise on the Unity of God is a prelude to his conceptual framework of the distinctiveness of man in the phenomenal world. Saadia stresses the Absolute in contrast to the numerical unity of God. Absolute Unity denotes the Uniqueness of God reflected in the initiation of a new notion of man as the embodiment of a margin of sovereignty in the universe, and a new relation between God and man as challenge and response and not as cause and effect. God's Absolute Unity in Judaism was, thus, in contrast to the multiple gods whose arbitrary powers reduced the position of man to a marionette dancing to the tunes of the gods.[12]

The third and tenth treatises on the observance of the Divine Law and ethical behavior are concomitants of Saadia's major focus on the process of human development in which the soul of the religious and virtuous person rises to ever loftier levels of authentication. The goal is for the rational faculty to control the activities connected with the lower faculties. What reason pronounces as valid behavior is ethically acceptable.[13] By the same token, the practice of mitzvot and intellection over them — even the conventional precepts — provide specific means for refining and ennobling our life's experiences and, in turn, for the growth and full development of our soul. Saadia held that reason discerns the basic goals of human action and *mitzvot* provide the best methods for actualizing these goals.[14]

Finally, the seventh, eighth and ninth treatises dealing with Resurrection, Redemption, Reward and Punishment are the eschatological extentions to Saadia's concern with the destiny of man. The classical work of Saadia is, thus, not a disjointed collection of philosophical notions incorporated from alien sources in an eclectic manner but an authentically motivated, well-organized volume with a variety of philosophical notions organically bound to a central affirmation.

b. SOLOMON IBN GABIROL

Solomon ibn Gabirol (1021-1058), the first Jewish philosopher in Spain, begins his magnum opus, *Mekor Hayyim,* with the master addressing his pupil as follows: "Inasmuch as by virtue of your native endowments and diligence you have acquired abundant knowledge in the study of the philosophic discipline, you may proceed to inquire about matters close to your heart, and especially about the supreme question concerning the aim of human life, why was man created?"

מכיון שהודות לכשרונותיך הטבעיים ולשקידתך עשית חיל
רב כל כך בלימוד החכמה, התחילה נא לשאלני על העניינים הקרובים
ללבך יותר, ובלבד שתגיע בהמשך השיחה אל השאלה החשובה
ביותר והיא : למה נוצר האדם?

His discussion on creation and substance is also calculated to delineate man as a universe in miniature comparing God's relationship to the world to that of man's soul and body. Especially significant is Ibn Gabirol's personalistic scheme on the epistemological level. Knowledge of God's unity depends on man's perspective. In God, essence and will are one. From man's vantage point, however, the will is identical with God if we think of it apart from its activity; considered as active, the will is an attribute distinct from divine essence. It is, then, from man's frame of reference that a determination is made whether essence and attribute are one.

c. MAIMONIDES

The three books of Maimonides' (1135-1204), magnum opus *Moreh Nebukhim* are similarly organically bound by a conceptual framework that is indigenous to his philosophy of Judaism. It is one integrated volume, imbued with the central thesis formulated in the first chapter of the first book which, to my mind, is an introduction to the entire book. In this chapter, Maimonides posits the primacy of man in the Bible by pointing out that the terms *zelem* and *demuth,* which have reference to the divine intellectual faculty, apply not to God's qualities but to man's. The Torah (in the creation episode) came to affirm man's unique quality "of the divine intellect attached to him," but not to describe "the Supreme Being as corporeal, having a material form." When the Torah says, *"Naase adam b'zalmainu kidmoteinu"* ("Let us make man in our image and our likeness"), it does not intend to compare God's image of man and thus introduce a doctrine of the corporeality of God which may be accepted. The reverse is the case: "I mean because of the divine intellect conjoined with man, that it is said of the latter, that he is in the image of God and in his likeness, not that God is a body and possesses a shape." It is interesting to note that Saadia also interprets *zelem* in its literal sense, although his general explanation of the biblical verse is different (*Emunot v'Deot,* 2, 9).

The major concern of the Torah is not to describe God's attributes but man's, in the sense of projecting man as possessing "as his proporium something that is strange, not found in anything else existing under the sphere of the moon, namely, intellectual apprehension" (*The Guide* 1, 1). It is, indeed, noteworthy that instead of introducing in the first chapter his theory of homonymous expressions, which constitutes the content of almost the first fifty chapters — and surely this would have been a fitting preface — Maimonides posits the terms *zelem* and *demuth* as absolutes pertaining to man's intellectual apprehension, and linked to the divine intellect. The attributes *zelem* and *demuth* in a logical sense apply equally to God and man. The Torah, according to Maimonides, came to posit the primacy of man and pointed to man's highest faculty attributes, and it is because of this intellectual faculty that it is said of man, "In the image of God created He him." This chapter is, then, an introduction to the entire *Guide* and, by the same token, it gives us an insight into the central role of man in the biblical methodology.

By the same token, toward the end of *The Guide,* Maimonides insists that God's challenge cannot be separated from its human counterpart. The nature of the challenge is, in part, what man brings to the encounter. In reference to the biblical verse "And I will hide my face from them and they shall be devoured" (Deut. 31:17) Maimonides admonishes us "It is clear that we ourselves are the cause of this hiding of the face, and that the screen that separates us from God is of our own creation. This is the meaning of the words, 'And I will surely hide my face in that day' . . ." (*The Guide* 3:51).

Positing the primacy of man as a frame of reference for all inquiry, Maimonides' evaluation of prophecy, providence, the soul, eschatology, theodicy and the Book of Job is of special significance.[16] Prophecy is attained at the ultimate stage of the actualization of the transcendental intellectual process.[17] In that state of realization a new personality comes into being,[18] reflected in the attainment of a totally new life experience, which views existence from a transcendental vantage point. This is the way Maimonides described the transcendental drive leading to the ultimate form of prophecy: "His (man's) thoughts must be engaged in lofty matters; his attention directed to the knowledge of God . . . There must be an absence of the lower desires and appetites . . . and, in short, every pleasure connected with the sense of touch . . . A man who satisfies these conditions, whilst his fully developed imagination is in action, influenced by the Active Intellect according to his mental training — such a person will undoubtedly perceive nothing but things very extraordinary and Divine, and see nothing but God and His angels. His knowledge will only include that which is real knowledge . . ."[19]

Divine Providence is likewise achieved when man has reached the final position of intellectual excellence and the new horizon that comes with it. "Divine Providence is connected with Divine intellectual influence, and the same beings which are benefited by the latter so as to become intellectual, and to comprehend things comprehensible to rational beings, are also under the control of Divine Providence . . ."[20]

The ideal man's soul is delineated as a "form which knows and apprehends concepts that have no body . . . And it is to that form that Scripture refers to as our form, our likeness."[21] This form arises from "the possession of notions which lead to true metaphysical opinions as regards God. With this . . . man has obtained . . . the highest human perfection . . . which gives him immortality, and on its account he is called man."[22] In its actualized nature it now shares in the immutable truths of reason and life and unites its essence with the eternal process.

By the same token, eschatology is depicted as a new dimension of human existence endowed with a new horizon that comes with it. The perfected soul enters into a new supernal order of being which views existence beyond the natural order of space and time.

In his fifty-first chapter of the Third Book, Maimonides summarizes his conclusion on theodicy in the following manner: "If man frees his thoughts from wordly matters, obtains knowledge of God in the right way, and rejoices in that knowledge, it is impossible that any kind of evil should befall him while he is with God, and God with him. When he does not meditate on God, when he is separated from God, then God is also separated from him; then he is exposed to any evil that might befall him; for it is only that intellectual link with God that secures the presence of Providence and protection from evil accident."

In this light, Maimonides interprets the Book of Job (*ibid.*, 22). The Bible describes Job as a good, virtuous man, fearful of God when tragedy befell him. But the text does not say that he was an intelligent, wise or clever man. It was only after he had attained a measure of enlightenment, wisdom and the realization that man's highest good lies in an intellectual fellowship with God that his affliction came to an end. In the ultimate situation, when man's encounter is rooted in an intellectual fellowship with God-in-Essence, he is finally relieved of all the accidents of time and space.

d. GERSONIDES

When we examine the major work of Gersonides (1288-1344) *Milhamot Adonai*, we note that most expositors maintain that the work does not represent a formulation of a complete, self-contained philosophical system, but is rather a treatment of certain specific problems which allegedly have not been treated adequately by Maimonides or have not been resolved to Gersonides' satisfaction.[23]

   This surely cannot be the case with a major work like the
Milhamot Adonai, which has been compared to both Maimonides' *Guide* and Aristotle's work in terms of critical analysis,
rigorous logical precision, and technical exposition. Many of
Gersonides' works were even translated into Latin, and their
fame extended far and wide.

   Why, then, should we assume that his major work was
not a comprehensive philosophic treatise. It seems to me that
when we examine the methodical way he divided his work,
we shall discover that his first treatise, on the psychology and
the immortality of the soul, posits the leitmotif of his philosophy,
and that the other five treatises revolve around his central theme,
each one projecting an authentic systematic philosophy of
Judaism. When a Jewish philosopher establishes a primary
datum that is authentically Hebraic and offers an adequate
treatment in support of his thesis, he writes with a sense of
purpose and direction as a Jewish philosopher.

e. CRESCAS

   By the same token, Crescas (1340-1410) starts his work
Or Adonai with praise to the Lord for having created man "as
a composite of all existence, inasmuch as he was formed from
all parts of existent things. Everything was subject to the rule
of his wisdom as well as to Divine rule. For this reason the
ancients, peace be unto them, referred to man as a microcosm,
for they regarded him as a miniature mold and seal embracing
all creation. It is, therefore, incumbent upon man to worship
Him and become attached to Him, which should be our
ultimate aim."[24]

כאמרו יתברך — נעשה אדם בצלמינו כדמותינו נשתתף עם
כלל הנמצאות בזה להיות האדם מחוקה מכל חלקי המציאות, והיותו

תחת ממשלת שכלו כאשר כל חלקי המציאות תחת ממשלת השם
יתברך, ולזה מה שקראוהו קדמוננו עליהם השלום עולם קטן כי שמוהו
דפוס קטן וחותם מחוקים בו כל יצירותיו כלם . . . לעבדו ולדבקה
בו אשר הוא תכלית האנושות.

NOTES

WHAT IS JEWISH ABOUT JEWISH PHILOSOPHY

(pp. 9-35)

1. See H. Malter, "Shem Tob ben Joseph Palaquera," *J.Q.R.* n.s. vol. 1, no. 2, p. 157.

It should be pointed out, however, that a sound point of departure for a Hebraic ideological construct—apart from Western secular philosophy and Islamic and scholastic theological formulations—lies basically in the classic Jewish tradition grounded in biblical and rabbinic sources. (Cf. L. Stitskin, *Judaism As a Philosophy*, pp. 218-226).

Curiously, the eminent founder of 20th century existentialism Karl Jaspers in his essay "Is Science Evil?" maintains that the Bible was also a major factor helping to shape the character of science. The rise of modern science is scarcely conceivable without its impetus. Three of the motives that have spurred research and inquiry seem to have come from it: (1) "The ethos of Biblical religion demanded truthfulness at all costs. As a result, truthfulness became a supreme value and at the same time was pushed to the point where it became a serious problem. The truthfulness demanded by God forbade making the search for knowledge a game or amusement, an aristocratic leisure activity. It was a serious affair, a calling in which everything was at stake."

(2) "The world is the creation of God. And if the world is the creation of God, then everything that exists is worth knowing, just because it is God's creation; there is nothing that ought not to be known and comprehended. To know is to reflect upon God's thought . . . The knowledge of the createdness of all worldly things replaces indifference in the face of the flux of reality with limitless questioning, an insatiable spirit of inquiry."

(3) "The reality of this world is full of tragedy. "That's the way things are," is what man must truthfully say. If, however, God is the world's creator, then he is responsible for His creation. The question of justifying God's way becomes with Job a struggle with the divine for the knowledge of reality. God's existence is undisputed and just because of this the struggle arises. It would cease if faith were extinguished.

This God, with His unconditional demand for truthfulness, refuses to be grasped through illusions. In the Bible he condemns the theologians who wish to console and comfort Job with dogmas and sophisms. This God insists upon science, whose content always seems to bring forth an indictment of Him. Thus we have the adventure of knowledge, the furtherance of unrestricted knowledge—and at the same time, a timidity, an awe in the face of it. There was an inner tension to be observed in many scientists of the past century, as if they heard: God's will is unconfined inquiry, inquiry is in the service of God— and at the same time; it is an encroachment of God's domain, all shall not be revealed.

This struggle goes hand in hand with the struggle of the man of science against all that he holds most dear, his ideals, his beliefs; they must be proven, newly verified, or else transformed. Since God could not be believed in if He were not able to withstand all the questions arising from the facts of reality, and since the seeking of God involved the painful sacrifice of all illusions, so true inquiry is the struggle against all personal desires and expectations" (*Commentary,* vol. 9, March 1950).

2. At the turn of the century with the rise of the quantum theory there emerged an unprecedented burst of theoretical and experimental findings that have revolutionized our ideas about the structure of matter and physics itself. Contemporary science has demonstrated that it is not the elements, but only the relations between them that are constant.

3. In the personalistic framework, however, the relational conception of the human personality is in its immediate situation of the hierarchical process. In the ultimate situation, personality alone has the characteristic necessary to a basal unity which constitutes its ontological reality. In this sense, the empirical scientist requires the underpinning of an ontological reality in which the ultimate substantiality and dynamic efficiency of existence is reflected.

4. The Bible already refers to those two categories of reason. The Psalmist speaks of *resihit hokhmah yirat Hashem* (Ps. 111, 10), the first principle of reason is to use it as an instrument of reverence for God. The Book of Proverbs, on the other hand, alludes to an ontological content of reason. *Reishit hokhmah keneih hokhmah*—the first principle of reason is to acquire reason (Prov. 4, 7). In the initial stage, critical reason employed as an instrument with which to probe man's essential nature draws man existentially to embrace the idea of God as the promise of our freedom. In the ultimate stage, reason as its own source of knowledge (hypostatized reason) necessarily validates the existence of God by cognitively identifying with Supreme Thought.

It is interesting to note that a contemporary Spanish philosopher, José Ortega Gasset delineates the nature of reason in a similar manner,

Asserting that human life is itself prophetic, for it is directed toward the future and bears the seeds of the future within itself, he asks: what will the future be like? It will not be, he replies, the logical, timeless reason of the Greeks, not the objective reason of science but rather a *vital reason* concerned with the ultimate horizon of the human condition, and with life not as it can be seen from the outside but as it is lived from within (*Man and Crisis*, tr. from the Spanish by Mildred Adams, New York, W. W. Norton & C., 1958).

5. The doctrinal implications inherent in this scheme are as challenging as the philosophy itself. Consider, for instance, the conception of God. The built-in hierarchical plan in man's condition projecting an ascending scale of perfection from possibility to realizability, requires not only that we seek the highest perfection but a belief that it is realizable. This cannot be without a Supreme Being who is the embodiment of perfection and eternity, and thereby the promise of its realizability. The human condition would fall into contradiction with itself if there were no God. To satisfy the demands of the essential character of our transcendent nature as a *zelem elokim* we are unequivocally driven into a conviction of the reality of a God Who is the guarantor of the actualization of our divine potential.

By the same token, the notion of the eternal destiny of the soul as a disembodied pure form is reinforced by the logical argument that the very nature of the transcendent nature of man's spirit would fall into a contradiction with itself if it did not possess an immortal core. For the human condition requires, not only to seek the highest and absolute self-perfection, but to believe that it is realizable in an ultimate cognitive kinship with the highest intelligence. As thought continues to shed all sensuous qualities of natural objects and converts them into concepts or essences, it finally apprehends God's existence as the ultimate abstraction with whom man establishes a cognitive identification.

6. To be sure, Spinoza's category of relation as substance, which establishes a naturalistic pantheism, is in contrast to the idealistic type which identifies God with the universal essence of being. While pantheism does not say that God is in everything, it maintains that God is the substance of everything and, consequently, there is no substantial freedom in anything finite and in so doing denies the freedom of God.

8. One of the oldest attempts to demonstrate the reality of God was the cosmological proof from the nature of the world which originated with Aristotle's doctrine of the four kinds of causes. We find that everything that happens around us comes into being as the result of the activity of other things. These activities, in turn, are themselves the result of other causes and so on in a causal series which must be either infinite or have a first cause which is not itself caused by

any preceding activity or member. But since we must exclude the possibility of an infinite regress of causes — such a causal series cannot "go back to infinity" and remain eternally inconclusive, inasmuch as to trace back the causal sequence endlessly, there would be no beginning to the series; and if there were no beginning there could be no succession, since each cause must follow after its predecessor — we must conclude that there is a first or uncaused cause responsible for the initiation of the series of events which we call God. (Aristotle's proof from the fact of motion inferring a first mover is basically similar).

The weakness of the cosmological argument lies in the difficulty of accepting an assumption of the impossibility of an infinite regress of events requiring no beginning. Indeed, David Hume thought that proofs from the nature of the world are *a priori*, implying that their conclusions — that the world could not bring itself into existence and that there is a source of existence outside the universe always in existence itself—are assumed in the very statement of the argument. Beyond this, Hume's general critique of causality (that every event must have a cause) rejected the fundamental premise of the cosmological proof. From his analysis there is no reason to conclude that the sequence of constantly conjoined events must have a cause to account for the effect. We can only determine what events occur in regular sequences with other events in our experience. But why must we conclude that the succession of these events have had a beginning?

9. The teleological argument purports to establish God's existence from the character of the natural World. The argument occurs in philosophical treatises from Plato's *Timaeus* to Saadia's *Emunot v'Deot*, Aquinas' *Summa Theologica*, Hume's *Dialogues on Natural Religion* and W. Paley's famous exposition in his *Natural Theology*.

The argument which causes us to regard the universe as a great machine gained momentum as an outgrowth of the modern scientific mechanistic accounts of physical phenomena, as for example Newton's mechanistic account of planetary motion. Nature, it is asserted, is not a mere jumble of accidents, a mere chance collection of parts, but as machine-like, all the parts fit together in one vast machine. Every thing in this gigantic order of nature conforms to pattern and is governed by law, just as the formation and assembling of many parts in a functioning machine necessitates the presence of a structure and pattern.

Paley's (1743-1805) analogy of the watch conveys the essence of the argument. Suppose that while walking in the desert we see a rock on the road. We can readily attribute its presence to chance, to such natural forces as wind, rain, heat, and volcanic action. But suppose we see a watch on the ground consisting of a complex structure of wheels, cogs, axles, springs, and balances all operating to provide a regular measure of the lapse of time. Surely we cannot attribute this orderly operation to the chance operation of wind or rain. We are obliged to postulate an intelligent mind which is responsible for the phenomenon.

Now if the natural world is a complex mechanism, an interesting analogy follows. It must have been made. Just as a watch implies the existence of a watchmaker, the existence of a universe-machine, which reveals an orderliness in the features of the physical, chemical, and biological aspects of the world whose complex structures function together in a co-ordinated system, implies the existence of a universe-machine maker, a designer or architect whose purpose it was to create this machine.

Hume's criticism of the argument from design is first levelled against the central claim and its fundamental contention that since there is a resemblance between effects of human planning and natural effects, the same applies to the cause of human artifacts and the universal causal agency. If we assume thus that like effects prove like causes and that the more similar the effects are the more similar are the causes, then we would have no ground to accept the traditional religious conclusions about the nature of God, such as infinity, absolute perfection or the moral attributes of the designer of nature.

Another difficulty lies in the very analogy between the universe and a machine. One could equally liken it to an animal or to a vegetable. But in this case the design argument fails. For like the animal or vegetable world, the entire natural world may possess some built-in seeds for growth as one finds in carrot seeds that orders the direction of their development. "The world," he says, "plainly resembles more an animal or vegetable than it does a watch or a knitting-loom." Its cause, therefore, may be some innate principle of development and order than an intelligent and conscious architect of nature.

Finally, Hume suggests that the Epicurean hypothesis that projects a universe consisting of a finite number of particles in random motion, which in due course after going through every combination possible for them arrives at an orderly cosmos, may have the same appearance of being designed as the traditional postulate of a deliberate, conscious designer. The same applies to other naturalistic explanations of the world.

10. The ontological argument which constitutes a proof from the nature or the idea of God was first developed by Anselm (1033-1109) in his *Proslogion* and later used by Descartes and even by a naturalist like Spinoza.

The argument begins by defining God in the way we talk about Him as an all-perfect Being containing all conceivable perfections, including the property of existence. The idea of absolute perfection being non-existent is self-contradictory for, not to exist is not to be an absolutely perfect being. It is an imperfection not to exist. The very definition of God as "that Being than which none greater can be conceived" guarantees His existence just as the definition or essence of a triangle necessarily implies three sides. Moreover, by the very definition of God as the Supreme Being, God must exist in reality, independently of my ideas, or else something greater than God can be conceived, since it is greater to exist both as an idea and a real thing than merely to exist as an idea.

The ontological argument considered as a purely *a priori* demonstration was rejected by several philosophers. A contemporary of Anselm in the Middle Ages, Gaunilon, pointed out that if this sort of reasoning of establishing God's existence from his definition of God were legitimate, one could also demonstrate that all kinds of imaginary or unreal objects such as a perfect island somewhere beyond man's reach must exist since existence necessarily follows the concept of perfection. St. Thomas Aquinas levelled his criticism against the assumption that we can know the nature of God, that He is a perfect Being, before knowing whether He existed. Actually the opposite is true. We must first establish His existence by other means and then proceed to define his properties. The most telling criticism of the ontological argument was advanced by Kant who rejected the basic assumption that existence, like triangularity, is a predicate which something can have or lack, and which may be analytically connected with a subject. Does the idea of existence enlarge or add anything to the concept of a particular thing as a predicate or property like blue or square adds to the idea we have of anything. If we conceive of something and then conceive of it as existing, is our idea of the thing any different? An imaginary hundred dollars, for example, consists of the same number of dollars as a real hundred dollars. Its monetary value that can be broken down into one hundred one dollar bills or coins is the same as a concept in my mind or as money in my pocket. The concept is the same whether one merely thinks of it or thinks of it as existing. Hence, the property of existence cannot be part of the concept of the all-perfect Being anymore than the existence of the one hundred dollars can be derived from one's concept of a hundred dollars. Existence is not a predicate or quality that enlarges a concept and cannot be part of any concept.

11. It is indeed noteworthy that the ultra-wordly theologians of the sixties, of whom Harvey Cox of the *Secular City* became the most fashionable champion arguing that modern man is no longer interested in the mystery of life but in the pragmatic solution of particular

problems, has recently published a book *Turning East*, in which he expounds the theory that American East-turners have merely coopted the vocabulary and outward trappings of Eastern cults and used them to reinforce the classical metaphysical preoccupation with self-identity and self-actualization. Alas, the search for the ultimate meaning of existence, as a renaissance of spirituality, is sorely needed by a people desicated by technological materialism.

12. Curiously, this notion is often grounded in the classical dialectic between thesis and antithesis. In life itself, it is argued, there is born the drive toward repeated self-destruction—not as self-immolation, but in order to arise again and ever again in a process that is to be continued infinitely. The continuous, unceasing reciprocal action of the absurd and creative commitment is part of the universal process that is the dialectic between life and death.

13. This notion of separation finds its counterpart in contemporary psychology, which maintains that the dynamics of the abstract attitude on the transcendental process are generated by the detachment and distancing of the immediate stimulus situation. The initial prerequisite for intellectual functioning, conceptualization, is to have the ability to transcend the binding attachment of the stimulus.

Cf. Kurt Goldstein, *The Organism*, New York: American Book Co., 1939.

NOTES

1. ISAAC ISRAELI

(pp. 36-56)

1. Knowledge of the truth, understood as theoretical knowledge leading to right action as its by-product, precipitates the process of self-transcendence and self-actualization, culminating in a cognitive identification with the Universal Intellect.

2. An article by Ibn Juljul (second half of 10th century) in the *Generations of the Physicians* (ed. F. Sayyid, Cairo, 1955, p. 87), is probably the first principal source of Israeli's life. Among the principal data of his life, the author mentions that he was a native of Egypt. He emigrated to al-Qayrawan and became a disciple of Ishaq ibn Imran and served as a physician of Ubayd Allah the Shiite . . . He lived to an age of over a hundred, never married and had no children.

He is the author of various works, the likes of which had never been written by previous writers, such as his book on urine, on fevers, on foodstuffs and drugs. He also wrote several books on philosophy, such as the book which bears the title of *Garden of Wisdom* and deals with questions of philosophy and metaphysics; his book on definitions and descriptions: his introduction to logic; the book on the elements.

When he was asked: Would you like to have a child? he answered: No, as I have a much better thing in the *Book of Fevers* — meaning and descriptions: his introduction to logic; the book on the elements.

A second biographical note on Israeli appeared in the eleventh century by Said of Toledo in the chapter on the Jews in his *Generations of the Nations* (ed. Cheikho, Beirut, 1912, p. 88). It is doubtless taken from Ibn Juljul but contained no additional information that Ishaq died shortly before the year 320 (932 CE). S. Fried in the introduction to his edition of the *Book of Elements* (Drohobycz, 1900) speaks of a later date. At any rate his pupil Dunash ibn Tamim refers to his teacher Israeli as no longer among the living in 955. We may thus assume that since he lived over a hundred years, his date of birth should be about 850.

The biographical information in later Hebrew authors such as Isaac Latters (in A. Neubauer, Medieval Jewish Chronicles, Oxford, 1895-11. 233-4) and Gedaliah ibn Yahya, *The Chain of Tradition*, Venice, 1586, fol. 40a is based also on the previous works. A comprehensive biographical sketch of Israeli's life, works and influence is given by S. Fried, who edited his *Das Buch uber die Elemente*, Frankfurt a.M., 1900. (See also Altmann & Stern, *Isaac Israeli*, Oxford, 1958 for an analysis of Israeli profile.

3. Isaac Husik, *A History of Medieval Jewish Philosophy*, New York, 1959 and Julius Guttmann, *Philosophy of Islam*, New York, 1964 present a summary of the major findings of Jacob Guttmann. David Neumark, *Toldot Hafilosofia be Yisrael*, Vol. 2, Philadelphia, 1929, however, opposes the conclusion reached by Guttmann that Israeli was basically a neoplatonist.

4. Other works on Al Kindi are Flugel's biography *Abhandlugen fur die Kunde des Morgenlandes* 1, Leipzig, 1857, M. Guidi and R. Walzen, *Studi su Al Kindi*, Rome 1940, Henry Malter, "Al Kindi" *H.U.C.A.*, Cincinnati, 1904.

5. See also Steinschneider, *Monatschrift*, 1893-4, p. 39; *Die Arab. Literatur Juden* p. 315; *J.Q.R.* 9, p. 62.

6. The *Ihwan al-Safa* interpreted self-knowledge in the sense of the microcosm motif. This is different from stating that the definition of philosophy as self-knowledge which Israeli sees in the soul of man as not only a microcosm but an actual participant in the universal intellect (*Ihwan* 14, 4, *Anthropologie* pp. 41-42).

Cf. Dieterici, *Mikrokosmus*, pp. 148 ff.

7. Unlike Al Kindi who lists six definitions of philosophy, Israeli mentions only two descriptions based on the etymological connoton of the term 'philosophy' as love of wisdom. 'Love' is identified with the ontology of the philosophic enterprise reflecting man's striving for authentic existence by understanding the truth of things on the basis of the four Aristotelian causes. When we know the cause of anything we know its essence and existence. 'Wisdom' is described epistemologically as self-knowledge.

8. Following Al-Rasi, Israeli delineates three internal senses, imagination, cognition and memory in his *Book of Elements, The Book of Definitions*, and the *Book of Spirit and Soul*.

The imagination operates on sensible forms of corporeal objects after these forms have been transmitted by the common sense and is thus dependent on sense perception.

The cognitive sense is defined in the *Book of Definitions* as an intellectual faculty "on account of which every cognitive being becomes and intelligent being." This notion, says Wolfson ("Isaac Israeli on the Internal Senses," *Jewish Studies in Memory of George A. Kohut*, ed. by Salo B. Baron and A. Marx, New York, 1935, p. 587), reflects the Aristotelian concept that "falsity and truth are not in things . . . but in thought" (*Metaph.* 6, 4). The dynamics of the cognitive faculty is described in the *Book of Elements* as the power of judgment, of analysis and of synthesis. In the *Book of Spirit and Soul* (*Sefer ha-Ruah v'ha-Nefesh*, ed. by Steinschneider, *Ha Karmiel* 1 (1871-72), 202) Israeli delineates the faculty as "perception and investigation, analysis, synthesis and consideration of the truth of things." This again parallels Aristotelian notions in *Metaphysics* (18-19, 29-30), that reason "is the faculty where truth and falsity exist, and they depend upon combination and separation." In *De Anima* (3,3), he further states that "truth or falsehood is something we judge" (Wolfson, *op. cit.* 591).

As to memory — the third internal sense — Israeli lists four definitions. In the *Book of Elements,* he describes the faculty of memory as "when the imagination receives sense images from the common sense, it conveys it to the memory" (2, 55).

In the *Book of Definitions,* he defines memory as (a) "The essence of memory in the mediation of things born in the soul by contemplation and investigation. (b) The purpose of memory is recovery of a forgotten thing and (c) the essence of preservation in the memory, without interruption" (*Definitions,* p. 139). Wolfson quotes from the work of John Damascinus, an Aristotelian Philosopher, as the source for Israeli's four definitions (Wolfson, *op. cit.* 594-95).

9. Cf. M. Steinschneider, *Heb. Ub.,* 479. Also *Die Arabische Literatur der Juden,* Frankfurt, 1902.

10. See Guttmann, *Die Scholastic des dreizenter Jahrhunderts in ihren Bezienungen zum Judentuum und zur Judischen Literatur,* Breslau, 1902.

11. Published in *Omnia Opera Yssac,* Lyons, 1515.

12. The passages in which Israeli is quoted by Magnus are collected by J. Guttmann *loc cit.,* pp. 55-60, and those of Thomas Aquinas by the same author, *Das Verhaltniss des Thomas von Aquino zum Judentuum und zur Judentuum und zur judischen* Literatur, Gottingen, 1891, p. 15.

13. See L. Stitskin, *Letters of Maimonides,* Yeshiva University Press, New York, 1977, p. 135.

14. Cf. Vajde, *Commentaire.* CVII, p. 20 and S. M. Stern, "A treatise on the armillory spheres by Dunash ibn Tamim." *Homenaji a Millas Vallicrosa,* Barcelona 1956.

"When he (viz. Saadya) lived in al-Fayyum, before he went to Baghdad, he addressed numerous letters to our city of al-Qayrawan, to our master, Isaac the son of Solomon, of blessed memory, consulting him about problems of the "external sciences" (i.e. philosophical and scientific — in contrast to theological — subjects). Rabbi Isaac used to show me those letters, though I was only twenty years old, and I pointed out some errors in them, which caused my master great pleasure, on account of my youth. Saadya left Egypt in the year 905." This passage also shows that Israeli died not later than 344/955-6.

15. See Altmann and Stern, *Isaac Israeli,* Oxford Press, 1958, p. 217. In my book *Jewish Philosophy: A Study in Personalism,* I have shown the Talmudic source (T. B. Yoma 67b) for Saadia's division

between rational and conventional laws:

ת"ר את משפטי תעשו (ויקרא י"ח) דברים שאלמלא לא נכתבו דין
הוא שיכתבו. ואלו הן, עכו"ם וגלוי עריות ושפיכת דמים וגזל וברכת
השם. ואת חקתי תשמרו, דברים שהשטן משיב עליהן, ואלו הן, אכילת
חזיר ולבישת שעטנז, וחליצת יבמה וטהרת מצורע, ושעיר משתלח.
ושמא תאמר מעשה תוהו הם ת"ל אני ה', אני ה' חקקתי ואין לך
רשות להרהר בהן.

16. Cf. Aristotle, *Posterior Analytica*, 2, 1. He enumerates four
types of inquiry: (1) whether a thing has a certain attribute (2) why
it has a certain attribute; (3) where a thing exists; (4) what a thing is.
Cf. Ibn Gabirol, *Mekor Hayyim*, 5.

כי הנמצא מסודר מהקצה העליון אל הקצה התחתון על ארבע מדרגות
והם, המציאות, והמהות, והאכות, והלמות.

17. Aristotle, *Topics*, 1,8. 103b. 15.

18. Israeli speaks of two kinds of causes — spiritual and material.
This is drawn from *The Life of Plotinus* by Porphyry, which is found at
the beginning of all complete editions of the *Enneads*. In Chapter
twenty-three Porphyry claims tnat Plotinus "lifted himself to the all-
transcendent divinity" by the method Plato teaches in *The Banquet*
wherein Socrates retails the words of Diotima, the wise woman of
Montinaea. The method taught there is that of a twofold purgation of
the mind, one qualitative; the other quantitative. The qualitative consists in a successive transposing of the object of one's thought to a
plane progressively more immaterial and spiritual, more completely
disengaged from the sense realm, more closely allied to the intelligible;
three levels of knowing that correspond to three levels of life; physical
beauty, moral beauty, intellectual beauty being the objects respectively
of the body, of those parts of the soul ruled by the ethical virtues, and
finally of the intelligence, that "eye of the soul," destined to contemplation. The quantitative purgation, in turn, consists in the progressive
detachment from the singular, from all the individualities that may
characterize this or that object loved; in a separation, that is from the
changing and the incidental in order to attach oneself to an object
that is immovable, essential fixed (as quoted by Elmer O'Brien, *The
Essential Plotinus*, The New American Library, p. 16).

19. Israeli delineates here another aspect of ethical awareness for
those whose theoretical knowledge does not intuit these rational precepts. They required a revealed ethics as communicated by the prophets and the sages.

20. The Latin translation reads *est longae profunditatis et sublimus
intellegenciae* "of great profundity and sublime intelligence." The
Hebrew version by Nissum and edited by Hirschfeld appears to be
erroneous, unless we translate it closely to mean 'devoid of any conceivable error.'

2. BAHYA IBN PAKUDA

(pp. 57-66)

1. The translation by I. Broyde has recently been published in a new edition in Israel.

2. *M. G. W. J.,* XLI, p. 241 ff.

3. In the introduction to his Arabic edition, edited 1907. Also Husik and Julius Guttmann concur with this opinion in their respective histories on Jewish philosophy.

4. A Zoroastrian sect descendants of the Persians who settled in India in the eighth century to escape Moselm persecution.

5. *TRADITION* — Vol. 7, No. 4.

6. Reinhold Neibhur, *The Nature and Destiny of Man.*

7. *Sefer Torot ha-Nefesh,* pp. 3-4.

8. Treatise 5 *Shaar ha behinah,* tr. M. Hyamson, p. 151.

9. The Persian philosopher al-Ghazali's (1059-1111) basic personalistic notions were regarded by Jewish philosophers as closely akin to those of Judaism. Yehuda, editor of the Arabic text of Bahya's *Duties of the Heart,* points out, for example, that many passages in Bahya's work are identical in content and expression with similar ones found in Ghazali's work. The latter's tolerance was reflected in his advice to his Islamic brethren to take the pious Jew as their prototype in religious spiritual reverence.

10. Psalms, 119:30.

11. *Ibid.,* 43.

12. The founder of the Mutazila (separatist) was Wasil ibn Ata, who in the eighth century separated himself from the school of the master and established a school of his own. The movement was based on two principles, freedom of will and the absolute unity of God, calling for a rejection of attributes

13. Abu Hashim 'Abd al-Salam, was the son of al-Djubbal, d. 321/933. He was a contemporary of al-Ash'ari, and one of the very last Mutazlia to exercise a direct influence on Sunni thought.

14. The works of Abu Hashim have not survived. He was known chiefly for his theories of "modes" (*ahwal*), a sort of conceptualism which attempted to resolve the problem of the relationship between the divine attributes and the divine essence. Anxious to safeguard the absolute Unity of God, Abu Hashim made use of the grammatical notion of *hal,* ("state" of the verb in relation to the agent), to define the degree of reality of mental concepts, and then the degree of reality of the divine attributes. The *hal* is the "state" established in our mind

by the meaning according to which the idea is received, and it is intermediate "between existence and non-existence." From the human concept to the divine attribute there is thus, for Abu Hashim, a constant interplay between the logical and the metaphysical. See *Encyclopaedia of Islam* V. 2, p. 125.

15. The founder of the Karaitic movement was Anan Ben David, born in Basra, Persia, about 714 c.e., who polemicized against the Rabbinic interpretation of Scriptures and denied the notion of *hasharat ha-nefesh.*

16. Bahya in linking partially Ibn Sina to Abu Hashim apparently accepted the common notion of explaining the semi-conceptualism or mysticism of the former as having been derived from Abu Hashim's thesis.

17. Ecclesiastes, 12:10.

3. ABRAHAM BAR HIYYA

(pp. 67-98)

1.   כי כל החלקים אשר החכמה נותנת להוציאם אל גוף המעשה
כבר יצאו מן הכח אל המעשה.

For a comprehensive study of Bar Hiyya, see my work: *Judaism As a
Philosophy. The Philosophy of Abraham bar Hiyya,* New York, 1960.

2. We may assume that Bar Hiyya probes the significance of
potentialities.

3. Cf. Maimonides, *Guide,* 1, 54. See also L. Stitskin, *Jewish
Philosophy—A Study in Personalism,* "Conception of God." pp. 306-12.

4. Ethics is not only concerned with the question, what is the
good? It also asks, how can I be good? How can I develop good
behavior patterns?

Modern philosophy tends to classify ethical theory into emotive,
non-naturalistic and naturalistic. A theory is defined as emotive if it
contends that moral judgments are neither true nor false but are
merely expressive of the feelings of those who utter them and arouse
the feeling of those who hear them. A theory is non-naturalistic if it
holds ethical judgments to be true or false but not reducible to any
natural science. An ethical theory is naturalistic if it holds both that
moral judgments are true and false and reducible to the concepts of
natural science.

5. The division of the world into periods based upon the days of
creation also provides a basis for a number of detailed calculations in
determining the date of the advent of the Messiah. See Guttmann,
Philosophies of Judaism, p. 114 for the source of this analogy. Bar Hiyya
further asserts that as a result of Adam's sin, knowledge and morality
descended from man's rational soul to the lower souls, thus losing its
independent power of development. Thereafter, only the elect in
every generation possessed the rational soul in its purity. It was only
after the patriarch Jacob that all his descendents shared a portion in it.

6. The reason for his detached and repetitive exposition on the
subject of forms is personalistic. It is to indicate that man's active
intellect is pure form similar to the moves of the spheres.

7. Time is dependent on existing things. It is a measure of the
celestial motions (*Sefer ha-Ibbur,* p. 3). It is not in another thing but
attached to the other thing and dependent on it. If time has a
beginning it also must reach an end. The book *Megillat ha-Megalleh* is
an investigation into eschatology—the end of time.

Bar Hiyya defines time here as an expression of the duration of
things in existence. For the seemingly variations in the two definitions

see my book: *Judaism As a Philosophy—The Philosophy of Abraham bar Hiyya,* pp. 99 to 103.

8. He wishes to indicate that the notions of hyle and form are reflected more authentically in the biblical expressions of *Tohu* and *Bohu.*

9. Bar Hiyya refers to the meaning of God's voice in the verse "And thou shalt return unto the Lord thy God and hearken unto his voice" (Deut. 30:2).

10. Bar Hiyya employs the term טעם in three different ways: (a) meaning — *Megillat ha-Megalleh* 49.; (b) proposition — *Sefer ha-Mishichah Veha-Tishboret* 11.8; (c) argument — *Sefer ha-Ibbur* 75.

11. The redemption of Israel will be marked by this transformation of the heart from a state of ability to choose between right and wrong, to a state of moving irrevocably to the right and of unremitting service of God. In *Megillat ha-Megalleh,* Bar Hiyya attempts to find through exegetic computation the year of redemption. He cites the following possibilities: 4790, 5118, 5208 (M.M. 46, 83, 107, 151).

12. Like other ancient and medieval philosophers, Bar Hiyya assumed that the heart was the seat of reason and understanding.

4. JOSEPH IBN ZADDIK

(pp. 99-107)

1. Cf. H. A. Wolfson, "Joseph Ibn Zaddik on Divine Attributes," *J.Q.R.*, ns. Vol. 55, no. 4, pp. 277-298. Also J. Haberman, "A Critical Note: Ibn Zaddik on Divine Attributes," *J.Q.R.* n.s. no. 4, pp. 308-311. Cf. I. Husik, *A History of Medieval Jewish Philosophy*, p. 146.

2. "Knowledge may be gained through sense and through intellect. Sense gives us the accident of things like color perceived through sight, taste through tasting, odor through smell and so on.

Such knowledge, say the philosophers, is only of the particular object. Only reason apprehends the universal and penetrates the essence of things. Consider as an example a book. The sense of sight perceives its color and through the color its form. This is then apprehended by the power of imagination located in the brain, which retains the impressions after the object has ceased to affect our senses. The power of imagination then hands it over to the cogitative power of the rational soul and from its reflection results the spiritual reality of the object, which is its knowledge. It is clear, then, that the rational soul knows the essence and reality of a thing whereas the senses know only the accidents, the vanishing qualities." Cf. Maimonides, *The Guide*, 1, 3. The term *Temunah* is used in the Bible in the same three different senses.

3. Stitskin, *Letters of Maimonides,* New York, Yeshiva University Press, 1977, p. 135, or *Iggerot*, Amsterdam, 1712, p. 146.

4. See Horovitz's *Der Mikrokosmos des Josef Ibn Saddik,* Breslau 1903. He is praised as a talmudic scholar by Moses Ibn Ezra.

5. A poem addressed to Yehudah Halevi about his visit to Cordova on his way to the Holy Land is included in the collection of Halevi's poems. Harizi and Ibn Daud praised the poetry of Ibn Zaddik.

6. See S. Horovitz, *Mikrokosmos,* 13, ff. Others like A. Jellinek in his edition of *Sefer Olam ha-Katon,* Leipzig, 1854 claim that Moses ibn Tibbon translated *Olam Katan* and cite as evidence a small poem at the end of the translation, composed by the translator which concludes with the words: לחזק ידי משה הכבדים.

A. Jellinek introduces his edition of Ibn Zaddik's treatise with the observation:

הספר היקר הזה העתיקו מערבי לעברי ר' משה אבן תבון, והוצאתיו
לאור זה פעם ראשונה.

As to whether Ibn Zaddik wrote an additional work of philosophy, there is a difference of opinion among scholars. In 1908 Moses S.

Junger edited a treatise *Sefer ha Musar* (Book of Ethics) by Ibn Zaddik, from a manuscript copy which belonged to Professor David Kaufmann and is now in the Oriental Library of the Hungarian Academy of Science. Prior to Dr. Junger's edition, Moritz Steinschneider discovered a similar fragment printed as an appendix to the rare edition of Jonah Gerondi's *Iggeret ha-Teshubah* published in Cracow in 1586, which he regarded as a part of the introduction to Ibn Zaddik's *Olam Katan* and not as an independent work. What led Steinschneider to this conclusion was the fact that Ibn Zaddik uses the identical short introductory laudation of God both in the *Olam Katan* and the *Sefer ha Musar*. G. Vajda in his study of Ibn Zaddik ("La philosophie et la theologie de Joseph ibn Caddiq" in *Archives d'Historie Doctrinale et Litteraire du Moyen Age,* vol. 17, 1949, pp. 93-181) does not mention the *Sefer ha-Musar.* Cf. J. Haberman, "A Note on the *Sefer ha-Musar* of Joseph ibn Zaddik" *J.Q.R.,* Vol. 55, no. 1, 1964.

5. MOSES IBN EZRA

(pp. 108-119)

1. The neo-Platonic scheme of emanation as we see it in Plotinus conceives of the universe as a process of successive descending gradations of being, preceded by a physical necessity as light from a luminous body, or water from an overflowing spring. At the top of the scale of cosmic existences is the One and the Good Absolute Cause Who is a strict unity and Whose nature is unknowable. Emanating from the Highest Existence is the second substance, the *Nous* or Reason, which is a duality of Thought and Being. From Intelligence proceeds a third hypostasis, the World-Soul which also has a dual aspect, the one spiritual by virtue of the intelligible world of which it is the last and the other, the material world of change and decay, called Nature, pertaining to the phenomenal world of which it is the first. Matter, too, is a duality, intelligible and sensible. The matter of the lower world is the corporeal, the non-existent, the indeterminate, and the capacity to pass from its potentiality to actuality. *Nous* (Reason), being an activity, has the underlying matter which has the faculty of being made determinate by the One. Man is also a duality. His body is material, partaking of the sensible world, of the evil of matter. His soul comes from the Universal Soul and if it is free from bodily contamination it will return to its home in the Intelligible world.

2.   See שער בפירוש השכל, p. 159.

3. Harizi rated his poetry as superior to that of Halevi.

6. ABRAHAM IBN EZRA

(pp. 119-133)

1. Ibn Ezra's small treatises include: *Sefer Hashem; Yesod Mora; Shaar ha-Shamayim; and Arugat ha-Hokhmah u-Pardes ha-Mezimah* See Meyer Waxman, *A History of Jewish Literature*, N.Y., 1960, Vol. 1, p. 339.

2. Cf. Ibn Ezra's concluding statements in his introduction to Ecclesiastes.

3. Like Philo he imputes to Eden the concept of the celestial world of divinity; to the Garden, the intermediate world of the Spheres and Intelligences; to the river, the substance of the sublunar world; to the fountainheads into which the river divides, the four elements of air, earth, fire, and water.

4. Some historians claim poverty as the reason for his travels.

5. נעשה אדם. דע כי כל מעשה בראשית לכבוד האדם נברא במצות השם. והצמחים, הוציאה אותם הארץ והמים וכל נפשות החיות. ואחר כן אמר השם למלאכים נעשה אדם, אנחנו נתעסק בו ולא המים והארץ . . . ובעבור שנשמת אדם העליונה שאינה מתה נמשלת בחיותה לשם, והיא מלאה כולו וגוף האדם כעולם קטן . . . וגם אמר הנביא, שראה כבוד אלוק' כמראה אדם.

6. והאדם לבדו הוא סוד זה העולם השפל ובעבורו נברא ונשמתו קשורה בנשמות העליונות.

7. ואמר בתחילה כי אין מותר לאדם מן הבהמה כי אם בנשמה העליונה החכמה, היא שתשוב אל השם הנכבד אשר נתנה.

8. כי אלה המצות אינם לצרכיו כי אם לטוב לנו כל הימים לחיותינו.

9. Yesod Mora, chapt. 7:

והמשל כמי שיגע עצמו ע"פ הרופא לבשל מאכל מה שיאכל שיועילנו והנה שבבריאתו ופעולתו בידו, והנה לטוב לך שתקבל שכר ותמלט מעונש, והנה הטוב הוא לאדם שמור מצות הרופא כי לא יועיל ולא יזיק הרופא כדברי אליהוא אם צדקת מה תתן לו ורבו פשעיך מה תעשה לו.

10. ובו תדבק', במחשבת הלב, שלא יעבור רגע בכל יכולתו שיחשב בלבו מעשה השם ונפלאותיו בעליונים ובשפלים ובתחתונים ובאותות הנביאים.

11. ונדעה נרדפה לדעת את ה'. ונדעה שנרדפה וכו' כי זה סוד כל החכמות ובעבור זה לבדו נברא האדם. רק לא יוכל לדעת את השם עד שילמוד חכמות הרבה שהם כמו סולם לעלות אל זאת המעלה העליונה. וטעם כשחר, כי בתחילה ידע המשכיל הש"י במעשיו כמו השחר בצאתו ורגע אחר רגע יגדל האור עד שיראה האמת

Cf. L. Stitskin, Jewish Philosophy: *A Study in Personalism*, pp. 305-309.

12. ולפי דעתי כי טעם פריו הנשמה החכמה שתהיה מלאה תורת
אלוק' להכיר בוראה ומעשיו העומדים לנצח, ותדבק בעולמה העליון
בהפרדה מעל גויתה, כמו הפרי המבושל באילן ויפרד ממנו. והנה נפש
הצדיק דומה אל הדגן שהוא עומד, והרשעים כתבן לפני רוח.

13. והנכון בעיני בעבור היות האדם נכבד מכל נבראי מטה אמר
כן. כי מעת שיחל הנער לדבר וזה טעם מפי עוללים אז תחל מתכונתו
לקבל כח הנשמה החכמה, עד שתשכיל בשיקול דעתה כח בוראה,
כי תחזק הנפש יום אחר יום . . . ,וכבוד והדר תעטרהו', בעבור כח
נשמת חיים שנפח בו שהיא עליונה ואיננה גוף על כן לא תמות.

14. שויתי — והנה נשמתו דבוקה בבורא טרם הפרדה מעל גויתה.
תודיעני — כי במות הגוף אז תודיעני דרך החיים. והטעם הדרך שאעלה
בה אל השמים להיות עם מלאכי עליון. וטעם שובע שמחות את פניך,
שיהנה מזיו שכינה. וטעם תודיעני, כי תאמץ הנשמה מעמסקי העולם
ותראה עין בעין האמת . . . והנה שכר הצדיק מפורש במזמור זה . . .
כי אחר שהוא דבק בכח עליון תעלוז נפשו וכח הדבקו בו . . . אני
בצדק — אין לי חפץ רק לחזות פניך, כי צדק ששמרתי היה סבה
להתענני כראות פניך . . . וזאת המחזה אינג' במראה העין רק במרא'
שקול הדעת שהם מראות אלוה' באמת. ואלה הדברים לא יבינם רק
מי שלמד חכמת הנפש.

15. והנה כל המצות על שלש דרכים. הא' באמונת הלב והשני בפה
והשלישי במעשה וכאשר האחד נמצא בכל חשבון ככה עקר כל מצוה
שהיא תלויה בפה או במעשה צריכה לאמונת הלב ואם לאו הכל
שוא ותהו ורז"ל אמרו רחמנא לבא בעי.

16. ומשה אדונינו אמר על כל המצות רק עם נבון וחכם הגוי הגדול
הזה ואם אין להם טעמים שנוכל לדעת מה טיבם איך יאמרו העמים
שהם חקים צדיקים ואנחנו השומרים אותם חכמים.

Cf. Ibn Daud, *Emunah Ramah*, introd. who uses this same verse to
indicate that Jews were always involved in philosophical pursuits. See
L. Stitskin, *Judaism as a Philosophy*, p. 221

17. See L. Stitskin, *Letters of Maimonides*, New York, 1977, pp.
156-157.

18. To know one's soul, according to Ibn Ezra, is the main
objective of philosophic speculation.

19. The mind is the most unique organ in the human body. It
is closest to us and yet furthest from us in the sense that it apprehends things that are so far removed.

7. SHEM TOB IBN FALAQUERA
(pp. 134-140)

1. Graetz, *Gesch.*, VII, p. 216.

2. Introduction: *Sefer ha-Nefesh*, Lemberg 1835. His prolific literary career included seventeen works. Three have been lost. Five are accessible only in manuscript. Nine have been printed.

3. See H. Malter on "Shem Tob ben Joseph ibn Palaquera," *J.Q.R.* N.S. Vol. 1 No. 2, p. 154.

4. However, one of the manuscripts of his books on Medicine, quoted in Ency. Judaica, Berlin, 1930 6, col. 904 on "Falaquera," implies that he had a son and presumably a wife.

5. *Deutsche Literaturzeitung*, 1894, p. 1637-8. Steinschneider quotes from 63 where Shem Tob recommends the practise of medicine as the "noblest of all human occupations." This was probably done in deference to his master Maimonies who was a physician.

6. Among his occasional poems he quotes a poet as deriding physicians who "kill off people and take their money. In this they have an advantage over the Angel of Death who must take the lives of people for nothing."

7. ראשית חכמה, published by M. David, 1902, p. 7.

8. Cf. H. Malter *op. cit.*, quotes the great German historian, Ranke who observed that the thirteenth century was the darkest in all human history. As for the Jews who were despised, harassed and branded with the yellow badge of degredation, Falaquera's following poem reflects feelingly the circumstances amid which he and his fellow Jews lived.

Can the forlorn Jew be joyous, Accursed is his lot among men? For, tho' today, his wealth be more Than sand upon the ocean's shore, Tomorrow goes he stripped and sore.	הישמח היהודי האומלל וחלקו בין בני אדם מקולל ואם היום יהי עשרו כחולים למחר יהלוך ערום ושולל.
What justice can there be for Jew His foe being judge and jury, too?	ומה יצדק ילוד יעקב ויזכה בעוד אויבו ידינהו ופלל
Or how should Israel raise his head, Wallowing in blood and sore-bestead?	ואיך ירים לראשו ישראל והנה הוא בדם מכות מגולל.
O God, redeem Thy people's state, And glorify and vindicate Thy name, which foes now desecrate!"	אלו־הים עמך הושע אשר אז תקדש את שמך המחולל!

9. ראשית הכמה p. 21 and המעלות p. 48. In one of his earliest
works, *The Treatise of the Controversy,* he tried to reconcile the study
of philosophy with Judaism. He argued that philosophical and scientific
investigations of truth are an essential part of the Torah. A person
who derived his belief in the existence of God from tradition alone is
inferior to one who gains such a belief through rational demonstra-
tions. The possibility always exists that through errors in the transmission of understanding of traditional views mistakes may develop,
and the knowledge imparted may be only partially correct. However,
a person who bases his faith upon philosophical proof of God's being
can be sure that his insights are completely true. (Treatise p. 6).
Hence, if one wished to gain a proper understanding of the Bible
and later rabbinic writings, he had to study Greek philosophy, which
Falaquera and other Jewish and non-Jewish savants maintained, had
originally derived from the teachings of Solomon and other Jewish
sages.

See H. Malter *op. cit.,* pp. 166, 167. Also L. Stitskin *Judaism As a
Philosophy,* Yeshiva University Press, 1960, pp. 218-226.

10. המעלות p. 11:

כדי להעיר הנפש משנת העצלה ולהזהירה תמיד על התמדה בלמוד
ולרדוף אחר המעלה העליונה שהיא מעלת החכמה.

11. Shem Tob, following Maimonides, distinguishes between the
Mutazila — the early Arabic expositors, who approached philosophic
notions with preconceived theological suppositions, and the later
philosophers Avicenna and Averroes, who pursued the philosophic
enterprise as an independent discipline. Cf. *Guide* Part I:71.

12. דעות הפילוסופים which was not published and is quoted by
Steinschneider, Cat. Leyden 65.

13. Falaquera makes a similar assertion in his introduction to
מורה המורה

14.   שמות רבה 10:1; היום אשר לא ידע את יוסף למחר הוא
עתיד לומר לא ידעתי את ה'.

8. HILLEL BEN SHMUEL
(pp. 141-153

1. Cf. R. Taylor, *Metaphysics*: "To think metaphysically is to think, without arbitrariness and dogmatism, on the most basic problems of existence. The problems are basic in the sense that they are fundamental, that much depends on them. Religion, for example, is not metaphysics; and yet if the metaphysical theory of materialism should be true, and it should thus be a fact that men have no souls, then much of religion would flounder on that fact."

2. In this respect we may regard the Maimonidean introduction of the homonyms as a major contribution to Jewish philosophy. Basically, the homonyms are an attempt to arrive at the meaning of ultimates from the perspective of man's existential position in the universe. They are expressions of the human condition confronting reality.

3. M. Steinschneider lists eight different manuscripts of *Tagmule ha Nefesh* in his letter to the editors of the *M'kize Nirdamim* attached to the printed edition of 1874.

4. What led Aristotle to his distinction of *nous* is the Aristotelian notion throughout that only motion can be an agent, which can make things happen and serve as an efficient cause. What then, he asks, makes us think? What actualizes certain universals at certain times? The *De Anima* is Aristotles' most systematic treatise. It is interesting to note that the phrase active intellect-*posetikos nous* — does not occur in Aristotle's work although passive intellect—*pathetikos nous* — does.

See Averroes, *Tahafut al Tahafut* — the First Discussion p. 14: "As for the thesis of a numerical plurality of immaterial souls, this is not a theory acknowledged by the philosophers for they regard matter as the cause of numerical plurality and form as the cause of congruity in numerical plurality. And that there should be numerical plurality without matter, having one unique form, is impossible. For in its description one individual can only be distinguished from another accidentally, as there is often another individual who participates in this description, but only through their matter do individuals differ in reality."

6. Thomas Aquinas anxious to combat this doctrine asserted that the active intellect is the highest part of the individual rational soul and that it requires no bodily organ.

Of special interest is the theory of Zabarella of the sixteenth century, Italian Aristotelian who distinguished between the souls sensible functions which are indissolubly united to the individual body and its knowing function when *nous* lifts itself to universals.

7. *Cf.* The Aristotelian definition of the soul as functional, unlike Plato who defines soul in his "Phaedo" in substantial terms. Activities determine the soul. Hence the central question about the soul as "the first entelechy of an organic body," is what faculties does it possess? What is it capable of bringing about?

Aristotle employs several analogies in his definition of the soul: just like the relation of the cutting of an ax to the ax, so is the relation of soul to the body. Or the relation of an eye to seeing: what makes an eye an eye, is its power to see. What makes a soul a soul, is its power, principle of growth, nutrition, self-reproduction and rational self-realization. The immateriality of knowledge makes the rational soul immortal.

8. Hillel ben Shmuel first presents the position of Averroes who held that there is only one universal soul and that its apparent multiplicity in different men is only accidental. One of the arguments Averroes advances is that if there are many souls, they are either eternal or created with the body. The first is impossible for since the soul is a form of the body, an infinite number of forms would necessitate an infinite number of bodies, otherwise the existence of these forms for the purpose of joining the bodies would be in vain. But it is false to assume that there has been from eternity an infinite number of bodies and yet they have not become real bodies with souls until now when form and matter are by their very nature always joined.

As to the second alternative of the souls created with the bodies, Averroes argued, we have two alternatives. They either came from nothing, or from something. From nothing is impossible for nothing comes from nothing, except by creation which is a miracle and miracles we may accept only through the dictates of our faith. The second alternative is also not feasible, for if soul comes from something, it must be from either matter or form. It cannot be matter, for form which is the actual and the superior cannot come from the potential and inferior. It cannot come from form for then it would proceed by way of generation and dissolution which is characteristic of matter not form. Hence we must conclude, says Averroes, that the soul is one in substance and number and it becomes many only accidentally by virtue of its receiving subjects like the light of one sun dividing into many rays.

As to evidence from the Bible, some expressions like the one in Genesis "And he breathed into his nostrils a living soul", the singular gender points to a unity of soul in substance and number while the prophetic verse . . . "And the souls I created" . . . indicates a multiplicity of souls.

Hillel then undertakes to strike a compromise by combining the Averroeistic scheme of a universal soul with neo-platonic notions of individual souls emanating from it in a descending series. The objection that forms cannot proceed from other forms by way of generation and dissolution Hillel asserts as invalid as indicated previously. "For we may respond to Averroes and say that the whole process of generation and dissolution is characteristic only of the action of body upon body which is by contact. A spiritual form however, which is a separate process is not identified with contact because it is not limited by time or place. We know that the Intelligences proceed from each other by way of emanation. From the act of self-contemplation emanates another separate intelligence.

From the act of contemplating its cause proceeds another sphere and the same thing applies to the soul. From one universal soul proceeds daily many individual souls. After death the rational part of every soul remains, that is the part which the soul receives from the Active Intellect through the medium of the *possible* intellect and returns eventually by degrees to the separate Intellect. This is the part which has the disposition in every individual to receive reward and punishment. In this manner we have adjudicated between the view that the soul is one and at the same time interpreted the biblical passages and hermeneutics which point to a multiplicity of individual souls, thus upholding the tradition of Israel by positing the salvation of individual souls and their reward and punishment.

9. *Tagmule ha-Nefesh*, 17 a

ואם יאמר אדם איך אפשר היות שהנפש בכללה היא צורת הגוף ועם
זה יהיה לה כח אחר מנפש שלא יהי' כח בגוף ולא צורת גוף. לזה
נשיב, אנחנו נראה בזאת בשאר הנמצאים כשנראה שום צורה שהיא
פועל הגוף מעורבת מן היסודות ועם כל זה יש לה שום כח אחר אותו
שאינו בה מכח שום יסוד חם או קר לח או יבש כמו שיש לאבן השואבת
כח למשוך הברזל ואבן פלוני לעצור הדם . . . כך יש לנו כוחות אחרות
נכבדים מעולים על מדריגת החומר . . . עם כל זה אינו מן הנמנע
הנמצא בה שום כח נפרד מעולה במדריגה שלא יהי' כח גופי ולא פועל
גופי ויפעול פעולה נפרדת וזהו השכל שהוא נפרד בעבור שאינו כח
בגוף ואעפ"י שהוא כח בנפש והנפש היא פועל הגוף.

10. Unlike Thomas, Hillel considers only the potential intellect a part of the individual soul while the active intellect he ascribes to the superpersonal character.

11. As the passive intellect conceives universals and ideas it becomes active and the more active it becomes, the higher it rises in the degree of conception until it conceives the active intellect itself and

becomes identified with it. This constitutes the process of conceptualization.

12. Kant's essential philosophical scheme underscores the same dichotomy between the mathematical scientific world which is characterized by causality and the inner life of man which when developed is characterized by freedom and oriented toward transcendence.

13. The response in this scheme of thought has its origin potentially in the very nature of the receiver. On the level of the intelligible, the actualization of potential intellect takes place not in the same manner of one body acting upon another which is by means of an efficient or material cause, but rather as its formal or final cause leading it to perfection. When Aristotle introduced the notion of four causes, he had this in mind, namely to grant the recipient a margin of subjectivity to choose, and strive for perfection. He is led on this course by the final cause endowing man with a divine spark that seeks actualization by drawing closer to Him.

While the corporeal response in man depends entirely upon external stimuli, the intellectual response is provoked by an inner drive to emulate its formal and final cause.

14. Medieval philosophy generallly addressed itself to two problems. Reason and revelation was the first concern of the medieval thinkers. Can human reason demonstrate theological beliefs based on revelation.

The second problem was the nature of reality and the relation between universals and particulars. How is common reality shared by individuals? Is supersensible reality expressible in human thought and language? To Plato, objects of thought are not found in objects of sense experience but we conceive them in our minds. Aristotle held that although we derive meaning in our minds, they refer to ordinary, particular objects.

15. We have here an interesting notion of *Torah lishmah* (knowledge for its own sake).

16. *T.N.*, p. 1b: The first proof he offers for the existence of the soul is that we see natural bodies take food, propogate their like, while others like stones do not take food, grow, or propogate their like. This shows clearly that the powers mentioned cannot be due to the corporeal part of the objects performing them, else stones, too, would have those powers as they are corporeal like the rest. There must therefore be in their being a different principle making for perfection other than a body which is responsible for those activities. We call it soul.

17. *Ibid.*, p. 2b: "The soul must be either a substance or an accident since all existents are so constituted. Now an accident according

to Aristotle is that which may be or not be without causing the being
or non-being of the object in which it is. But one cannot possibly
conceive that a body remain a living body without the soul. Hence the
soul is not an accident." In the Aristotelian tradition the soul by its
definition represents the boundary line between living and non-living.

18. *Ibid., pp.* 3b, 4a: After ruling out in section 2 the soul's union
and separation from the body as motions since descent and ascent
when applied to the soul are not a spatial relation, Hillel proceeds in
this section to reject the notion that the soul is subject to motion while
in the body. After enumerating Aristotle's six classifications of motion
such as genesis, decay, increase, diminution, qualitative change and
motion proper, he shows that the soul can have none of these motions.
As for the qualitative changes such as from joy to grief, "to this we
reply that these changes are not due to the soul but to certain corporeal
powers which are in a state of mixture of the humors in the body
and which the soul shares insofar as it is united with the body as
Galen indicates in all his medical works."

19. *Ibid.,* p. 7a: "The soul is a stage of emanation consisting of a
formal substance which subsists through its own perfection and occupies the fourth place next to the Active Intellect giving primary perfection to a natural body. Its ultimate source is God who is the true
Perfection and the ultimate Good and it emanates from Him through
the mediation of the Separate Intelligences standing above it in the
scale of emanation. Aristotle gives a similar definition of the soul as
the first entelechy of a natural body."

To be sure, we have here an extreme form of an Aristotelian neo-
platonized definition of the soul, which places the soul fourth in the
series of emanations. Even Ibn Zaddik's definition represented a purer
rendering of the Aristotelian standpoint. Apparently Hillel was not influenced even by Maimonides' definition. The reason may be that since
he translated part of the Proclean book *Liber de Causis* into Hebrew,
thinking that the author was Aristotle, he imbibed completely its neo-
Platonic content and ascribed it to Aristotle.

20. See Note 8.

21. *Ibid.,* p. 10a: "Just as the senses require three instruments to
realize their operations, so does the intellect. And the three elements
are: one, the power of reception, that is, a sensory organ. Two, an
external real object to arouse the sense faculty to perceive. Three, an
agent that will bring the object of sense perception to the senses, that
is the air which is the medium of transmission.

Similarly with regard to the material intellect, we have three grades
of intellect. First, the faculty of receptivity which is the material
intellect similar to the relation of the senses to the objects of sense

perception. Secondly, the faculty of acquisition, the capacity of the material intellect to apprehend the intellect. This is the speculative faculty (the actual functioning of the possible intellect), which is called the acquired intellect. Thirdly, the active intellect, which is the agent responsible for actualizing the material intellect.

22. *Ibid.*, p. 3b: This problem follows the pattern similar to the major issue of the treatise, namely, the unity of the human intellect. It arose from Averroes' interpretation of Aristotle's psychology in which he maintained that the intellect is a unitary immaterial substance and not a form of the body. On the other hand, the part of the soul which is associated with the body as its form embraces the lower faculties of sense, and dies with the death of the body. Hillel disagrees with Averroes and posits the possible intellect as part of the soul for reward and punishment. He cites as an example that when the soul experiences anxiety and other emotions the latter are reflected in the human intellect "and if the possible intellect were a distinct substance it would not be affected by the accidents of the soul" (*Ibid.*, 19b).

It should be noted that Thomas Aquinas maintained that the active intellect in the Aristotelian scheme was also part of the human soul— and not one of the separate Intelligences. Hence, the rational part too has an individual existence both during life and after death.

23. *Ibid.*, 20a-20b: After discussing the various opinions regarding the nature of reward and punishment, Hillel first advances a natural proof for the spiritual nature of reward and punishment. He argues that immaterial substances like the soul cannot be influenced by corporeal treatment. For corporeal influence implies motion on the part of the agent casting its influences upon every part of the recipient. But since a spiritual substance has no parts, it cannot therefore be subject to corporeal influence.

Moreover, from a purely practical standpoint, if retribution is corporeal, it would be more effective if it takes place on this earth where the soul is still joined with the corporeal body. The effect would be much greater also upon others, who would see how the righteous are rewarded and the wicked punished.

After a lengthy discourse on the nature of spiritual reward, in the second section, Hillel offers the doctrine of resurrection as further proof for spiritual retribution. If retribution were corporeal, he argues, why is it necessary to join body and soul together again after death for their proper compensation when the same purpose would have been served in one's lifetime (p. 24).

24. *Ibid.*, p. 26b:

הנה מצאנו שרבותינו ז"ל אמרו בכמה מקומות בתלמוד שגיהנם הוא
מאש חמרי ושנפש הרשע נשרפת באותה אש אחרי מותו . . . עשן

עולה מעל קברי רשעים לאלתר אחרי מותם...ומצאנו ג"כ שנפש
הצדיק היא מתענגת בנהרי אפרסמון טהור, ושלחנות של זהב בעלי
רגלים, ובגנת שיש בהם אילנות בעלי ריח ואפילו עליהם מופלגים בריח.

Hillel quotes many such passages where retribution is projected
in corporeal terms such as the wicked burning in fire and "smoke rises
from the grave of the wicked immediately after burial, while the souls
of the righteous delight in pure waters, golden tables and gardens filled
with fragrant trees." He proceeds to show that such passages are not
to be taken literally for the contents of the Talmud are divided in six
groupings, not all possessing the same binding power. The discussions
of Halakhah, which embraces legal and ceremonial laws as well as
narratives of miracles, must be taken literally. However, the parables
and allegories, peculiar *aggadot,* homilies addressed to the people on the
holidays for spiritual purposes, biblical interpretations where no ceremonial precept is involved, visions of the future in an allegorical
manner, jests by way of relief from the strain of study—all these cannot
be understood literally. Accordingly, retribution is expressed corporeally
in order to impress ordinary people with frightening punishment con-
sequent upon wrong-doing.

A KEY TO AN UNDERSTANDING OF THE MAJOR
PHILOSOPHERS

(pp. 154-166)

1. *Emunot,* Intro. 1.
2. *Ibid.,* 4, 1. tr. by S. Rosenblatt, New Haven, 1948.
3. *Ibid.,* 5, 1.
4. The first attempt to identify the sources of the various opposing theories was made by Jacob Guttmann, *Die Religions philosophie des Saadia,* Gottingen 1882, pp. 194-197, who attempted to trace them to the list Aristotle gives of earlier philosophers in the *DeAnima.*

Cf. S. Horovitz, *Die Psychologie bei den judischen Religions— Philosophen,* Breslau, 1898-1912, pp. 12-21.

Cf. H. Davidson, "Saadia's List of Theories of the Soul," *Jewish Medieval and Renaissance Studies,* ed. A. Altmann, Cambridge, 1967, pp. 75-94.

5. *Emunot,* 6.3.
6. S. Horovitz claims that the source for Saadia's position is Nemesius in *Nat. Hom.* p. 45 in the name of Eunomius, who referred to it as a combination of Plato and Atistotle. Interestingly Horovitz suggests that if one could posit an independent entelechy, one would understand Saadia's definition (*op. cit.,* p. 26, n. 43).

7. *Emunot,* 6.3.
8. *Ibid.,* Intro. 5.
9. *Ibid.,* Intro. 2.
10. Reproduced in Halberstam's edition of Judah B. Brazillais,' *Perish sefer Yezirah,* Berlin, 1885, pp. 70 ff.
11. Cf. T.B. Berakhot 10a. A similar note is found in Plotinus' *Enneades* 6, 5 and 6.
12. It is significant that Saadia's discussion of the attributes involves the way man experiences God in relation to him as the Creator. He writes: "Considering the subject further I found that the conception of God as Creator, which we established, implies the attributes of Life, Power and Wisdom. By means of our faculty of ratiocination, it becomes clear to us that creation is impossible without power and that power is impossible without life and that a well-ordered creation presupposes an intelligence which knows in advance the results of its activition . . . For the very idea that God is the Creator involves the attribution to him of Life, Power and Wisdom, as I explained" (Emunot 2,4).

Cf. A. Altmann, *Three Jewish Philosophers,* Philadelphia, 1961 p. 82 n.3.

13. *Emunot*, 10, 2.
14. *Ibid.*, 3,3.
15. *Mekor Hayyim*, (1:3).
16. For an examination of Revelation and The Conception of God, see my book *Jewish Philosophy: A Study in Personalism*, pp. 275, 306-309.
17. Maimonides, Introduction to *Haelek*, T. B. Sanhedrin.
18. "And the Spirit of the Lord will come mightily upon thee, and thou shalt prophesy with them, *and shalt be turned into another man*" (Sam. 10:6).
19. *The Guide*, 2.36.
20. *Ibid.*, 3, 17   .
21. Maimonides, *Yesodei ha-Torah* 4:8.
22. *The Guide*, 3, 54.
23. See I. Husik, *A History of Medieval Jewish Philosophy*, New York, 1930, p. 329.
24. While Yehuda Halevi's work is primarily a defense of religion and not a philosophical exposition—although to my mind his opposition to the philosophic discipline was directed mainly against the neoplatonism and especially its notion of the active intellect with which man ultimately establishes a relation instead of with God directly—to be sure his insistence that the observance of the mitzvah is adequate to establish such a relationship is another notion that distinguishes him from other Jewish philosophers.

However, the Kuzari is replete with many aspects of personalism. For instance the content of religion, Halevi argues, is not to teach the existence of God as a ruler of the Universe. This could be known by mere exercise of discursive reasoning. The distinguishing feature of religion is the conception of a close relationship between God and man. God's nearness to man is reflected in the biblical appelation of Y.H.W.H., denoting the personal nature and character of God, in contrast to *Elokim* which reflects the sum total of all forces controlling the universe.

Yehudah Halevi's formulation of the notion of *inyan Elohi* (*al-amar-al-ilahi*), is likewise an attempt to define this doctrine of the divine idea in the context of the degree divine activity manifests itself in each soul. Just as the rays of the sun are reflected in varying intensity, according to the nature of the objects receiving its light, so is the extent of the ramification of the *Inyan Elohi*, the unceasing, ever-sustaining divine activity dependent upon the nature of each soul. Hence it is the character of the soul that ultimately determines the manifestation of the Divine Presence.

Index

BIBLICAL REFERENCES

TALMUDIC REFERENCES

(References in Notes not listed)

HEBREW PHRASES

SUBJECTS AND NAMES

BY THE SAME AUTHOR

Judaism as a Religion

Judaism as a Philosophy: The Philosophy of Abraham bar Hiyya

Jewish Philosophy: a Study in Personalism

Letters of Maimonides

Studies in Torah Judaism

Studies in Judaica